Who You Were Meant to Be
Moshe Sharon

Discover your purpose
& dare to follow your dream

The day on which you were born was the day the Almighty decided that the world can't exist without you.

Attributed to Rabbi Israel ben Eliezer, the Baal Shem Tov

Who You Were Meant to Be

Moshe Sharon

Copyright © 2018 Moshe Sharon

Translation: Shalom Mashbaum
Contact: Sharon@mo6.co.il

ISBN 9781793486943

WHO YOU WERE MEANT TO BE

MOSHE SHARON

Contents

Foreword

I believe that each of us has a divine spark.

I believe that each one of us is unique and special, and that there's no one else like ourselves.

I believe that each of us came to the world with a certain gift, a gift that you can discover and actualize in the world.

I believe that each of us has come here with a role and our purpose is to leave the world in better shape, in one way or another, than it was in when we arrived.

I believe that everyone has the will and the desire, even if they are hidden, to leave behind a legacy, a gift of their own.

I believe that we all want, in one way or another, to make an impact.

I know from my experience that it's not always clear what that "gift" that we came to the world with is, or what our "role" in the world is. Our daily lives are full of events and episodes, circumstances, and tasks that we must complete, and we usually don't have the leisure time to deal with such a profound and significant question as "Why did I arrive in this world?"

But I also know that this is one of the most important questions a person should ask himself.

The answer to this question, in fact, defines what the mission or purpose of the person in the world is.

Many times, during my work, I meet people who raise

the question "Why did I come to this world?" This question frightens them. What frightens them more than the question itself is thinking about and pondering its implications. Usually, dealing with this question arouses many fears, some of which are known and others which are not, that we don't always want or aren't always able to deal with.

"If I know what my role in the world is, does that mean that I *have* to fulfill it?"

"And what if I can't?"

"Does that mean that I'll have to leave my job, or give up the source of my livelihood?"

"And is it possible that if I play my role, I won't have time to devote myself to my family, my children, or my hobbies and other activities?"

"And what will happen if I fail?"

In this book, Moshe Sharon gives a precise response to all these questions and uncertainties. By reading it and doing the exercises, you will learn how to identify your mission, and how to overcome your misgivings and your fear of failure.

When I got a copy of *Who You Were Meant to Be* from Moshe, the name of the book alone thrilled me. I really believe, as Moshe explains beautifully, that each one of us came to the world when they did for a reason.

For some reason, some people look at realizing our destiny and mission as a task that clashes with our everyday, routine existence, but things don't have to be so.

I embrace the notion that each person has to find the path that is most appropriate for them, through which they will both realize and implement their mission, and continuing to live their daily lives, in which all their wants, desires, and dreams come true.

Some people think that a person's mission must be a "super-mission," something in the order of "changing the world from one extreme to the other." We have become used to hearing and reading about remarkable people who took their talent, abilities, and ambition, and produced major inventions, or assumed prominent roles that influenced humanity.

Not all of us can see ourselves as being where these exceptional people are. Not all of us can see ourselves as the next Waze inventor or being appointed as the next prime minister, or being the next Nelson Mandela.

But to me, there is a positive message: We needn't all be the inventors of the next Waze. Our mission and destiny in the world needn't be realized precisely by leading countries, or by creating breakthrough technological inventions.

Each one of us, by using their talent, abilities, knowledge, and the experience they accumulate during their life, and by what they do, changes the world every day. **We really do this**, with or without bombastic newspaper headlines.

I have accompanied tens of thousands of people in the course of my work, and I met a great many who, through what they do, start by having an impact on their own close circle of people, their family and friends. And these people impact other people.

The truth is that we will never really know how much we impact the world, and we also will never know exactly whom we influenced and whom we helped. Sometimes, a word or sentence that we said to a certain person can permeate, influence and change that person's worldview, and then their activities, and from there this worldview affects all the circles of people affected by that person.

If each one of us works to realize their talent, abilities,

knowledge, and experience, we couldn't even describe how much they could impact the world.

Finding our job, finding the messenger in us, is a process. I think that this process doesn't really have a definite and absolute end. It's a process that begins on the day we were born, and will probably end on the day when we leave this world, but as we proceed we implement the gifts we have, and we become more precise and more influential.

You, who are holding this book now, have a role to play. You have a mission.

Do you need help to identify and implement your mission? Moshe created a practical guide for you that will lead you, step by step, through the process of identifying your mission and your role in the world, the path you're expected to take, and how to perform your mission.

You can expect to be led on an exciting path that will transform you - enjoy!

Eran Stern[1]

---

1   Eran Stern enables business owners to realize their business' purpose, and is the author of the Amazon bestseller *Fulfilling*.

FROM THE BEGINNING –
On a Personal Note

When I was in high school, I came across a poem that influenced me deeply. If my memory doesn't deceive me, it began:

You're reading too fast. Slow down for a moment. This is poetry.

It's hard to believe, but that line from a poem has left a real mark on me. That day, I decided to slow down. When I slowed down, I discovered how special and fascinating people are, how a whole world is folded up in each and every person.

I decided to study psychology, philosophy, sociology, anthropology, criminology, and, later on, Judaism in general and the wisdom of Kabbalah in particular. One day, I discovered coaching and training tools. After I studied these tools thoroughly, I realized how much coaching is a practical tool that helps people to make their mark on the world, to feel and be significant. And when you connect coaching with the wisdom of the Torah and spiritual studies, you get an atom bomb that can change one's life, and the life of all of us here on the face of the Earth, dramatically.

This is because helping a person find their purpose in the world is an art, the art of empowering the other.

It's an art that has no limits. It can help CEOs realize the dreams they put aside for many years, for the sake of their career, and, equally, it can help anyone connect to what they do many hours a day.

"Meaning" can help all of us put ourselves in our right place.

It's an art that helps a person to emerge from their own fixed template, from the boundaries they themselves have set, and to mark new boundaries. It helps them to stop preventing themselves from being what they could have been, and what they wanted to be. It's an art that abandons judgmentalism and restrictive guidance. The answers are found within the person themselves. Not with me. Not with an outside consultant.

There is a story about the Baal Shem Tov, the founder of the Hassidic movement, that he would get letters at home with questions. He didn't answer the questions directly; he would just erase the unnecessary words in the question and send it back. That way he showed the questioner that the answer is embedded within the question.

It's an art that helps a person to enjoy the potential of the future instead of crying about past failures. It's the art of listening to others and not to oneself. It's the art of asking the correct question. This art helps a person to become even better at what they do best, instead of spending so much energy on being someone else. It's the art of being the person I would most want to be.

It's time to stop this crazy flow of life and treat myself like a gentle treasure, like someone who must go as far as they can. To stop speeding through life so fast that I have no time left to really enjoy it. To slow down for a minute. To allow poetry to burst forth. To allow the inner melody to play.

To ask myself only one question:

What do I really want to be?

In my experience, working with quite a few people who were seeking their purpose, I discovered that every person is at a different distance from the answer. They range from total ignorance to complete knowledge.

This book will frustrate some people quite a bit, even though in it I suggest practical ways to discover their purpose and destiny. Why? Because deep within themselves, while they concede that there is a need to discover their mission, the search is hard for them, and despite their efforts, they don't manage to find what they're looking for. These people may very well need a personal guide, as the Sages say: a prisoner doesn't release himself from prison on his own.

There are those who are very close to their mission, and this book will give them the final stamp of approval, and send them on a path full of challenges and satisfaction.

Some people have already discovered their purpose and will smile broadly. For them, the book will reinforce what they already know and have experienced.

In any event, it was a great privilege for me to write this guide and help people find their purpose. For, as Rabbi Israel Salanter said: We are not innovating anything. Our work is only to illuminate what is hidden deep inside the person.

It's a great privilege — because it seems to me that leaving my own private mark on the world is nothing in comparison to something much more significant — helping others make their mark on the world.

'If you're reading this guide, I'm privileged and delighted it has reached you. And if it will also help you to connect to your mission in the world, I'm delighted many times over.

If so, right now, our joint work begins:

a. To help you connect to the idea of a mission.
b. To find out exactly what your mission is.
c. To translate the insights we discover in everyday reality.
d. To offer solutions for the fears that arise in some of you.

I wish you success. Don't worry; I'm with you all the way.

Introduction

Every man is a genius, but if you judge a fish by its ability to climb a tree, it would live its whole life believing it was stupid.

Albert Einstein

Take a break for a moment from the loads of things you're doing, go to the park or to a nearby outdoor café, sit on a far-off bench, and look at the people around you: what do you see?

A businessman rushing to a meeting, a mother strolling with her children, a school-aged child on their way to school, a man schlepping bags of groceries, a city sanitation worker cleaning the street, a boy and a girl on their first romantic date.

What do they want? What motivates them? Why did they leave their homes? Why do they get up every day to face a complex and sometimes exhausting reality?

Many psychologists, philosophers, and clergymen would give this question a seemingly simple answer:

Humans are motivated by a variety of needs — from basic survival needs (food, sleep, etc.), through security needs (political, economic, medical, etc.) to needs of belonging, recognition, social status, and more.

The 20th-century Jewish-American psychologist Abraham

Maslow, described this as a pyramid of needs: when a lower need in the pyramid is satisfied, the person becomes free to develop and satisfy higher needs such as art, self-knowledge, and other things — needs that cannot be found in our partners on the planet, the animal world.

As we know, no chicken will give up its portion of grain to go to a concert.

But if we ponder for a moment the *depths* of people's *needs* to find out what they really want, what motivates them from within themselves and not just on the surface, we will find that *they want to be meaningful.*

From one point of view – to be meaningful to parents and family, spouses and the children, friends, the environment, and so forth. The need to be meaningful is a human necessity so basic that if a person feels that no one cares about their existence; their personality will degenerate into fear, anxiety, resentment, hatred, evil, despair, and other maladies.

Humans need the feeling that someone loves them, believes in them, thinks about them, cares about them. Not for nothing did Rabbi Carlebach express himself as follows: all a child needs is one adult who believes in him.

From another point of view — the desire to be meaningful is also reflected in the realization of one's uniqueness, of one's self-empowerment, in a person's desire to bring to fruition a talent they have, in a desire to leave a mark. People want to feel valuable, to feel that they are needed, that their life isn't merely a fleeting shadow. They need to feel that "they were here," that they didn't live in vain, that their opinion is important and given recognition, that their uniqueness is also recognized, that their talents are valuable and admired, that what they give is lovingly accepted.

Rabbi Ashlag asks a question which hits the mark:

> What is our role in the long chain of reality, of which we are only tiny links?

(Introduction to The Zohar)

Or simply put: If so many people have lived here in this world in the past, and so many more will in the future, what do we ourselves add? What unique value do our lives have?

Is it true that everyone is searching to be meaningful? Everyone without exception?

Dealing with the subject of "mission" raises some important, real questions that I am asked every time I have a heart-to-heart discussion with someone about the importance of the subject.

First question: Who says that the idea of a mission is something that suits everyone? Maybe it's not right for me.

Indeed? Is it plausible that mission or destiny is a concept that applies to only some of the people in the world? That a mission, a destiny or leaving a mark is a luxury for the rest of the people who live and work in the world?

If so, we would have to ask why people bother to leave behind a memorial, a tombstone, a book, stories of heroism?

Why do people donate to a charitable institution and request that a plaque be hung up there with their name on it in huge letters?

Why do people want to be written on the pages of history?

Why do people leave wills that convey a message to their descendants?

In other words, if all people die at some point, why do they need to leave a mark after their death?

It's told about members of the Zionist youth movements in Krakow, Poland during the Second World War that they rebelled against the Germans, even though they knew in advance that the chances of winning were nil. Their leader, Aaron "Dolek" Liebeskind told them in November 1942:

> We are fighting for three lines in history, so that it won't be said that our youth went to their death as lambs to the slaughter.

There's a story about Sostratus, the architect who designed one of the Seven Wonders of the World, the Lighthouse of Alexandria, at the request of King Ptolemy II. The architect wanted his name to remain on the lighthouse for generations, and to be remembered as the one who designed it, but he knew that the King would kill him if he dared to commemorate *his* name on the lighthouse, instead of glorifying the name of the King. What did he do? He engraved his name on a marble plaque in the lighthouse, and then put a layer of lime over it, on which he engraved the name of the king. In the course of the generations, the wind, rain, and sun wore down the layer of lime, and the name of Sostratus was exposed to the world in all its splendor.

The answer to the first question is: Since there's no one who doesn't want to feel significant, and since there's no person who doesn't have a unique talent they wish to express, from this we can see that the idea of mission or destiny relates to *every* person, and every person performs their mission differently. Everyone without exception.

Everyone?

Yes, indeed. A mark isn't only a place of honor in the pages of history, and not just anybody outstanding such as Maimonides leaves a mark.

It seems that the most basic mark we leave on the world is our children. The poet Dahlia Ravikovitch was quoted in the *Yedioth Aharonot* newspaper as saying:

> The birth of my son, Ido, was the happiest and most lasting experience I ever had. Through him, I discovered eternity. I think that anyone who has children has a part in eternity.

Yediot Aharonot "7 Days" supplement. August 26, 2005

Indeed it seems that the birth of children is the basic and most readily available way to tie ourselves to eternity, and thereby deal with the finiteness of life.

The Book of Genesis describes this as follows:

> And He expelled Adam [...] And Adam knew Eve his wife, and she conceived and bore Cain, and she said: "I have acquired a man from God."

(Genesis 3:24-4:1)

The moment Adam and Eve were expelled from Paradise and lost eternity, they chose to give birth to Cain, an eternal "acquisition."

Another example from the Jewish sources can be found in the words of the prophet Isaiah:

> Thus the Lord said to the eunuchs: [...] and I have given
> them a memorial... better than sons and daughters. I will
> give an eternal name that will not be cut off.

(Isaiah 56:4-5)

God, who knows that the eunuchs are desperate because they can't have children, promises them that if they keep His commandments, He will give them a connection to eternity — an eternal name.

Rabbi Eliyahu Dessler writes:

> Everyone desires children... because he regards his chil-
> dren as a continuation of his being, after he has departed
> from the world.

Michtav M'Eliyahu ("Letter from Eliyahu")

The story of the binding of Isaac also expresses the need of every person to leave a mark on the world through his children. Abraham and Sarah waited for a child for decades; they shed so many tears. When Isaac was born, God promised Sarah and Abraham that a great heritage would come from this child, and He blessed them and the child.

When Isaac reached the age of thirty-seven, God turned to Abraham and said to him:

> Take your son, your only son, whom you love, Isaac, and
> go to the land of Moriah, and offer him there as a burnt
> offering. (Genesis 22:2)

In effect, God allows Avraham to test himself and his level of faith: will Abraham argue with Him "Wait, you promised that a great people would emerge from me, like the stars of heaven" or would he without question forsake the blessing he was promised, and sacrifice his son with his own hands?

When God discovered that Abraham was *prepared* to sacrifice Isaac, even though it was clear to everyone that the demand to sacrifice him was in stark contradiction to the promise he was given, and even though murder stands in stark contrast to Abraham's whole worldview, God sent an angel to say to Abraham:

> *God forbid,*
> *Do not lay a hand on the boy.*

There's no need to do so. The test was to see whether Abraham would be *prepared to sacrifice*.

Fighting over the Mark

How many times do couples find themselves arguing about "whom does our child resemble — you or me?" Why is it so important to them that the toddler be like one of them?

Why does it matter if the genes of humans pass to their children, or not?

Why is it important to any person, be they the most open or liberal, that their children live according to their values?

Why do people experience some kind of anxiety when they think their continuity is "escaping" to a place other than the one they wished for?

If a person loves their children, they should be happy whatever they choose to be, and whatever mark they choose to leave, isn't that so?

And even if for a moment we set aside children as the basic

share a person has in eternity, we are still left with many typical human behaviors that demonstrate beyond any shadow of a doubt the need to leave a mark.

Anyone involved, for example, in municipal issues, is familiar with the recurrent battles which are waged in various municipalities, in Israel and around the world, regarding the issue of street names. Many families, whose loved ones have left a mark of one kind or another, go to fight for their name on a street. It seems that for the relatives of the departed, if a street isn't named after them, it's as if they never lived, as if they had never done anything that made an impact anyone.

Another example from the world of teenagers can be found at the end of high school. There, about six months before graduation, a handful of boys and girls get together and begin writing their collective memory, called "the yearbook." For the students, the question "What will they write about me?" or, in other words, "How will I be engraved in everyone's memory?" is an extremely fateful question.

The desire of people all over the world to publish books is also an expression of the strong desire to leave a mark. And the list of book writers is very long: politicians, painters, singers, sculptors, and doctors, as well as university researchers who invest decades of their lives in research, finding a new cure or scientific breakthrough — many of these people want to publish a book.

Why do the world's wealthiest people establish hospital departments in their name? Why establish a new department at a university named after someone?

Why has our need to document and perpetuate people grown in recent years? That this is so can be concluded, of course, from the boom in private electronic media storage, as well in the number of pictures that preserve the images of our children. The number of pictures taken of the average child in the Western world could easily compete with the number of those taken of presidents and prime ministers.

Even ordinary people, who aren't professors or famous, try to exploit their abilities and talents. Each of them tries to leave his fingerprints on the world.

So yes, everyone seems to be "sinning" in the desire to leave a mark.

Second question: I have to work to support myself and my family, when exactly am I supposed to find my destiny? Who has time for this?

"I don't have time!" the rabbit shouted to Alice in Wonderland.

I understand both the rabbit and the one who asked the question. We ourselves don't have time either — there really isn't enough time. Every adult living in Western culture is convinced that if they would only be given another hour every day, they would complete the endless tasks stacked on their desk. No time? Seventy years of existence, twenty-five thousand days to live and to do things — where are you hurrying to?

The answer is that time is always there, but it's limited. It will end. It, and we, will end.

We are finite, mortal; our bodies won't function forever.

If so, without being fully conscious of this fact, we are in a race — with time itself. Under the outer wrapping of 'some peoples' activity lies a feeling of anxiety that they will be forgotten, that their uniqueness will disappear, that their share in reality won't be preserved.

Even the belief in reincarnation, which unites almost all

religions in the world (I will say more on the subject of reincarnation in the next chapter), which expresses, among other things, man's human need to live in the belief that they and their loved ones remain here forever, if not on the physical level, at least on the level of the soul, isn't fully consoling.

In effect, once some people realize they are not eternal, ever since the moment of man's expulsion from Paradise, from the moment they realize that they are mortal, they look for any possible way to hold on to eternity.

So the answer to the second question is itself a question — **if not now, when?** In other words, you didn't come here to this world to "work" and "to make a living." These aren't ends in themselves. So throw out the newspaper, shut off the TV and set the smartphone to flight mode — it's worth it for you to take the time and thought needed to answer the question of mission. Anyone who needs help doing this should seek help from a coach or a psychologist, and so on. Whoever claims "I don't have time" is similar to the patient whose health is deteriorating but who continues to run around not treating their illness because they don't have "time" to see a doctor.

Third question: What will happen if I "go with the flow" without worrying about my mission? Can't I live a "good" life even without impressive, fancy words such as "mission" or "destiny"?

The answer is, no, not really, or at least not for long. As Maslow writes:

> If you intend to be something that is less than what you are capable of being, it's reasonable to believe that you will be miserable all your life.

For example, Odelia dreamed of becoming a doctor but didn't get into medical school, so she began looking for a different profession. All her friends recommended teaching, since it's great to raise children being a teacher: you come home early, you have good working conditions, and you have a number of days off that you won't find in any other profession. Odelia was accepted to a teaching program, and indeed became a teacher a few years later. Odelia doesn't really like what she does, but she flows with it. How long do you think Odelia can carry on without a sense of meaning? Until her pension? How long can you be cut off from yourself? Teaching without a sense of mission is not only doomed to failure, it probably won't last.

If you want to look at this idea from a wider perspective, you can examine it in light of the writings of the Grand Rabbi of Slonim, who claims in his Hassidic commentary on the Torah, "*Netivot Shalom*" ("*Paths of Peace*"):

> If someone did not fulfill the mission for which they descended into the world, that is, there's a unique mission for which he went down to the world, and not for another purpose, when he ascends to the upper world, they will ask him *what have you done in the world, if you haven't fulfilled the mission for which you descended*? So why did you go down to the world at all? To waste precious time?

Rabbi Moshe Chaim Luzzatto (Ramchal) opens his famous book "*Mesilat Yesharim*" ("*Path of the Just*") as follows:

> The foundation of piety, and the root of divine service, *is for the person to clarify and verify his duty in this world*, and at what he should direct his gaze and his efforts in all that he does in the course of his entire life.

This are his questions:

Why did you come here?

Do you know what your duty is in the world?

Why do you go to work every day and come home, go to work and come home, and once again go to work and come home? Why did you get married? Why did you bring children into the world? What's all this for? Why were you given eighty years of life? Why not twenty? Why not four hundred?

Even though our deepest desire is to find meaning, most people don't even ask what their lives mean.

The Greek philosopher Seneca understood this more than two thousand years ago:

> If a person does know towards which bay he or she is aiming, then every direction of the wind will be the right one.

Imagine the following conversation: You stop someone in the street and ask someone:

> Where are you going?
> To a nursing home.
> Where are you coming from?
> From work.
> Why are you going to a nursing home?
> To perform the *mitzvah* of honoring my parents.

It sounds like a sensible conversation. But if you asked him:

Where are you going?
Don't know.
Where are you coming from?
Don't know.
So why are you going where you're going?
Don't know.

You'd probably think he is a strange person and maybe needs help.

When you stop a person and ask him — where are you going? *No, not at this very moment*, but where are you going in the course of your life? Where will you be in two years? Or forty years from now? For what purpose do you live? Where do you want to get to?

Their answer might be "I don't know; I just want to survive, to get by."

And where did you come from?

Don't know. From the monkey?

And what's this whole undertaking of life for? What's the point?

I don't know, you live, you know, from minute to minute, day by day. You win some, you lose some.

The absurd thing is that a person who answers these questions in this way might be considered normal. *It is amazing that someone who doesn't try to find out where they are headed and why, is considered normal*

Someone who spends his time just putting out fires and surviving, just getting by, is considered normative?

I met Naomi at a point when she was frustrated and disgusted — "I'm sick of work" she told me.

She works five hours every day as a cleaning lady for a religious woman who has nine children. I, unlike her, was enthusiastic — "You help a mother of nine children? Wow! That's an awesome mission."

"Mission?" She didn't understand what came over me, why I was impressed.

"Yes, this mother, the one you work for, what does she say to you?"

"That I'm saving her life; I'm her angel."

"Well, that's what I thought."

"So why am I not happy and content?" she asked.

"There are two possibilities. Either you have a lot of talent that needs to be broadcast elsewhere, or you just think about how you're being forced, against your will, to make a living, instead of choosing to also see how tremendously much you're helping this family. You should be aware that you're doing things "'for a reason'," because without this realization, you're a messenger in deed only, but in your consciousness, the difficulty of earning a living makes you suffer. Yes. Your unhappiness is in your head."

So the answer to the third question is: Surely you can live without impressive, fancy words such as "mission," just as theoretically as you can live without love, but this "life" is bland, tasteless, deficient and merely survival-oriented. It's the kind of life that, in the end, people regret that they lived. Why live such a life? As Rabbi Nachman of Breslov said:

> I am now living the kind of life I never lived before. There are all kinds of lives; all of them are called lives, but I am now living a greater life than I have ever lived before.

Moharan 8

Or in simpler words, as in an ad I once came across: **The fact that you have a pulse doesn't mean that you're really alive.**

Fourth question: What does the knowledge that I'm significant or that there is meaning to my life give me?

Victor Frankl, a Jewish psychiatrist, who developed the psychiatric method logotherapy, and who experienced the horrors of a Nazi labor camp, argues in his book *Man's Search for Meaning* that survivors of concentration camps were those whose lives still had meaning, who felt that there was some mark on the world that they still felt they had to leave behind, or who had hope in their hearts to meet their loved ones again.

The sense of meaning, according to him, revived a person's hungry and sick body. He writes:

I remember a personal experience. I had terrible wounds on my legs because of the wetness of my shoes... I would stumble, together with a long line of people, from the camp to our place of work... I thought at that time about the innumerable little problems in our miserable lives. "What will we get to eat this evening? If we get another piece of sausage as an extra ration, maybe I'll exchange it for a piece of bread? And maybe I'll make a deal using the last cigarette I have left from a bonus I got two weeks ago, and offer it for a bowl of soup? How can I get a piece of wire, instead of the clip I used as a shoelace?..." I got sick of this situation, which forced me to reflect, day by day and hour by hour, only on tiny matters. I started to think about other subjects. Suddenly I saw myself standing on the podium in a nice, well-lit, warm lecture hall. An attentive audience was before me, sitting on comfortable, upholstered chairs. I lectured on "The Psychology of the Concentration Camp"! Everything that depressed me at that moment suddenly became objective, as if described from the distant point of view of science. Thus, I somehow managed to transcend my present situation, the sufferings of the moment, and thought about them as if they were a thing of the past. I and my troubles were transformed into the subject of a scientific, psychological study of myself.

Frankl, who survived because he presented his profession as a "doctor," cites Friedrich Nietzsche in his book, who claims that

Anyone who has a *why* to live for can endure anyhow.

Therefore, the answer to the fourth question is: Meaning gives a person tremendous power, especially when they are faced with difficulties.

Fifth question: I'm a religious Jew, and I thought that our role as Jews is *only* "to observe Torah and *mitzvot* (commandments)" and for this we receive "reward" or "punishment" — isn't that right?

This is a somewhat complex question, because the concept of Torah and *mitzvot* is so complex, with many distinctions and issues, but I will try, despite its complexity, to answer it: Rabbi Kook, one of the greatest Israeli leaders of our time, sees our mission as a condition for our creation and descent to this world: He quotes the prayer: My God, before I was created, I

was not deserving of creation, and now that I have been created, it is as if I had not been created.

This quotation is from the Yom Kippur prayers, and usually
we interpret it as a negative comment: it wasn't worth it for the
Lord to create me, and now that I was created, I continue to
sin and disappoint Him. Maybe it would have been better if I
hadn't been created at all.

Rabbi Kook understands this phrase completely differently:

> Before I was created, during all that unlimited time from
> the beginning of time until I was born, there must have
> been nothing in the world that needed me, because if
> something in the world had need of me, I would have
> been created. For example, if I had a role to play as one
> of the founders of the State of Israel, I certainly would
> have been born precisely during this period, and not only
> after its establishment and since I was not created until
> the time when I was born, this is the sign that I was not
> worthy of being created until then, and there was no need
> to create me before I was born. If so, why was I created
> now? *Because the time had come for me to accomplish
> something to complete reality.* A reality that, without me,
> and without my share, won't be complete; part of the
> puzzle would be missing without me.

(Olat Raiyah 2, p. 44)

Just a minute, why doesn't Rabbi Kook write that I was created
because the time had come for me to observe the commandments? There must be something more.

Let's look at another example:

It isn't only on Yom Kippur that our Sages remind us how

critical and precise our mission is, but also on the Jewish New Year, Rosh Hashana, as well. Most Jews know that they are judged on Rosh Hashana, judgment day. But what exactly are they judged on? Is it the transgressions and the *mitzvot* they have done in the last year?

The Grand Rabbi of Slonim, in his book *Netivot Shalom*, thinks otherwise:

> According to this, the subject of law and judgment on Rosh Hashana is clear, since today is the day of the rebirth of the world, this is the day on which the world is re-created, by pregnancy and rebirth, as it were, thus, every creature of the world will be brought to trial, there is a trial, as we know, for all creation, and what are they being tried for? What is the trial about?
>
> *There is discussion in Heaven whether or not they fulfilled the destiny and purpose that the Creator designated* and whether the good in the world overpowered the evil or vice versa, God forbid, because according to the secrets of creation, *every detail of creation has its own role and destiny within the overall purpose of creation*, it would not have been created; therefore, regarding the renewed creation, *there is a discussion whether this individual is needed for the coming new year as well, or if they are superfluous and unnecessary, and no need for them still exists.*

Netivot Shalom, Essays for the New Year

Simply put, *the answer to the fifth question* is: we are not judged about fulfilling commandments and avoiding transgressions; we are judged in regard to our purpose. Did we fulfill it, or not? Are we still needed, or, God forbid, not anymore?

If so, what's the role of the *mitzvot*, since they must be important, meaningful and binding? I will answer this later in the book, in the fifth insight.

Sixth question: You assume that everything has meaning. How do you know? Maybe nothing has meaning? Maybe it's all vanity?

The sixth question raises a deep and ancient issue that thinkers have dealt with for many generations: *Does everything in life, in reality, have meaning, or perhaps nothing has meaning?*

Is there, or isn't there, such a thing as things happening "purposelessly"? Is our existence here accidental, lacking any real value?

Or perhaps there's a "Supreme Intellect" (some call it cosmos, universe, or God) Who sent us here, who has given us a way, a mission, a certain direction?

King Solomon dealt with this question in the Book of Ecclesiastes. In the beginning of the book, he tells us how he obtained wisdom, money, and power; how he enjoyed all the pleasures of the world, and how he discovered that ultimately everything is "vanity of vanities," complete nonsense. Some of the people I met during my life, as well as some philosophers, especially existentialists, agree with the initial words of King Solomon, that everything is vanity, meaningless.

However, you will find that if you look at reality with the right eyes, ultimately, everything in the world has meaning, from a small harbor to the great ocean.

The beauty of Ecclesiastes is that King Solomon doesn't provide proof of meaning, but rather tells about his *personal* search. Why? Because the truthfulness of either meaning or meaninglessness *can't be proven*, just as it's impossible to prove the existence or non-existence of God. The answer to the question is that *of the searcher*. And the implications of the answer are far-reaching.

This is actually the answer to the sixth question: You decide. Your answer can lead you to a place where you value and cherish every little detail of the reality of your life, because if a person decides that there's meaning to life, then every detail of their life has meaning, and there isn't even one detail that's superfluous or worthless.

On the other hand, choosing the model of an accidental reality, which claims randomness and lack of meaning, can make you cynical, devoid of faith, and a skeptic.

Rabbi Yehuda Ashlag, author of the commentary *HaSulam*) *The Ladder*) on the Jewish mystical work the *Zohar*, asks about the meaning of life as follows:

> What is the point of our lives? In other words, the years of our lives, which cost us dearly in light of the suffering and pain that we undergo in order to complete them to their end who benefits from them?

Introduction to The Study of the Ten Spheres

Is there a point to life, beyond the pleasures of physical life, which are visible to the eye and sweet to the palate? Are the lust for life and the fleeting moments of happiness we enjoy worth the suffering and tribulations that we undergo?

There are, of course, many other questions, such as "how will I know what my mission is," and "who says that what I think about my mission really is true and accurate?" and other such questions. Don't worry — I will answer them in the following chapters.

FIVE
INSIGHTS

FIRST INSIGHT

THE MISSION IS ALWAYS DIRECTED TOWARDS OTHERS

A rich Hasid went broke and went to his teacher, Rabbi Shneur Zalman of Liadi, to tell him of his woes: he needs money to pay off his debts, he owes money for tuition, he has to marry off a daughter, he has to rejuvenate his business, and similar things that people need. The Rebbe looked the Hasid straight in the eye and said to him: "Your honor has told me in detail what he needs; I'm surprised that he never asked himself for a second why is he needed in the universe?"

Simcha Raz, Tales of the Righteous, p. 26

When a man or woman is drafted into the army, at the first stage the army will usually be mixed them in with all the new enlistees. As part of a large group, the new soldier will be given basic training, which will wipe out their uniqueness, abilities, and skills. The army will make the new soldiers always be on time, and hassle them with middle-of-the-night assignments and pointless, Sisyphean roll calls completely unconnected to their job in the army.

After the first stage, which lasts for at least a month, the system will start to train each and every soldier for a special assignment. One will be trained as a sniper, someone else as a lookout. These training sessions are designed to build up the individual, as much as possible, in the framework of the available time and the army's needs.

In the third stage, the army will use the soldier's skills according to its always- changing needs.

This description sounds obvious and natural to anyone who has ever served in the army, but if we look at things more broadly, with a zoom-out to universal existence, we can ask ourselves a very profound question: do people, from the moment they're born, also undergo a similar "soldier-making" process? Does the universe, similar to a well-arranged and organized military system, train each and every one of us for a needed role? Are all of us, despite our sense of individuality and freedom, in effect "drafted"?

This question is, of course, too profound to answer by means of regular, commonplace tools. We will therefore have to make a use of the principles of Jewish mysticism.

How the Wheel Turns

According to Jewish wisdom of kabbalah, no human being in the world has a unique soul.

If so, what is a soul?

There is **only one unique soul**, which is called "the soul of Adam, the first human being." This soul, born as a result of the sin (of eating from the Tree of Knowledge), was shattered into six hundred thousand slivers, and afterward into more and more fragments.

Each of us, according to this conception, is made up of a material body and a divine part, a fragment of that soul.

We have a unique connection to that one, inclusive soul. It's a common mistake to say "I have a soul." It's more accurate to say "the soul has me."

Or, in Rav Kook's words,

> The individual doesn't have a soul; rather, it is derived from the entire people.

(Shmona Kvatzim (Eight Collections), I, 161)

From time to time I'm asked, does "transmigration of the souls" exist according to the Torah and the Sages, or is it just an idea that believers from other cultures or religions, such as Indian or Druze, believe in?

The answer is that, yes, the special sliver of each of us, part of the whole, a part which no one has except for me, transmigrates again and again, every time into another body.

Rabbi Yehuda Ashlag explains:

> Even though we see the bodies, which replace one another as they pass from generation to generation, this is only what happens to the bodies. But the souls, which are the essence of the body, do not die or disappear from the world like the body, but are copied from body to body throughout the generations… in such a way that *here in our world, there are no new souls*, as there are new bodies, but a certain number of souls transmigrate and clothe themselves, each time in a new body and a new generation. Therefore, if we look at the spiritual essence, all the generations, from the beginning of time to the final redemption, should be regarded as one long generation, which lived for several thousand years, until it was brought to its intended fruition. *And*

it is not important at all that in the meantime, everyone replaces their body thousands of times, because the essence of the body, which is called the soul, *did not suffer at all* from these replacements. There is in this matter wonderful wisdom, called "transmigration of the souls," which explains that every individual in the world lives eternal life. And even though we perceive through our senses that everything ultimately degenerates, this is only apparently, as we see things, but in truth there is nothing here but transmigration; each individual doesn't rest even for a moment, but rolls forward and doesn't lose even a bit of its essence in the course of its travels (like the **law of conservation of energy**.)

(from the essay "HaShalom")

In other words: You can imagine Adam as a type of body, from whom each one of us come, each from a different part of his body. One sliver is hewed from his arm, thus will be a valiant soldier, or someone good with his hands. Another sliver will be hewed from his heart, thus will be sensitive to other people, and so on.

Just as there are billions of cells in the body, so each of us is an individual cell from the universal soul which is called "Adam, the first human being."

As in the army and in a human body, no two cells are the same, and each cell's job is to serve the whole body.

Repairs (tikkunim), Ladies and Gentlemen, Repairs

Continuing the Kabbalistic description: after Adam's sin, we were expelled from the Garden of Eden, beginning a process which is supposed to take six thousand years (we are now in the year 5779 of the Jewish calendar; that means that there remain 1221 more years for the world as we know it, and in the year 6001 we will enter a new reality, which is called "the seventh millennium").

What are we supposed to do in this world for six thousand years? The answer is — undergo corrections, repairs, and transformations.

Repair something? What? What's broken?

Most of the people I know are put off by the word "*tikkun*," correction, repair; it seems to me that they regard it as a criticism, as if we're all incorrigible and corrupt.

In general, we can say that all of us are undergoing the same *tikkun*, correction or repair, because if there was one Adam and all of us are slivers of him, then *the correction, the repair of all of us is to return to the situation in which we live with a unified, inseparable consciousness*; to return to be one body.

This is the reason why the Sages tell us of a potential convert who came to Hillel, the wise Rabbi, and asked him to learn all the entire Torah on one foot. Hillel answered -

What is hateful to you, do not do to your friends (and the rest of the Torah? Go and learn!)

Is this the entire Torah?

Of course not.

Rather, the main job of every individual in the world, is connected *to their relationship to all the other slivers*. I will expand on this immediately.

If so, when we come to use the word *tikkun,* we must understand precisely its two meanings:

1. *Repairing our relationship with others from egoism to altruism.* That is, there's nothing broken in us, what's broken is how we relate to others, to everything outside of ourselves, for in fact the "other" is part of us, and not really something separate.

2. *Tikkun in the sense of "installation" (Hebrew: hatkana).* Just as we install new software on a computer, so we are expected to install new software on the "**heart of the person, which is evil from his youth**" (Genesis 8:21). Or perhaps it's more accurate to say, this is really the old, original software, and I have to return to the root, to the source from which reality began.

What about Me? I didn't Come Here to Repair Myself!

Isn't it possible that I arrived in the world in order to learn something about myself? To experience? To live? To survive? It seems that the answer is clear: just as the purpose of the heart isn't to maintain itself, but rather the entire body, so too regarding the person: *the person's mission in life is always defined in relation to others, and not in relation to themselves.*

Just as the army trained you so that you can contribute, and not just so that you can develop yourself.

Even the well-known motto "a person must repair themselves," isn't precise.

It's more precise to say as follows: You can't repair your relationship to others unless you repair yourself and your character, unless you work on conceit, anger, envy, and so on.

No person arrives in the world just to repair themselves, *because repairing one's self is a means to performing carrying out one's purpose*, so that the person can be a trustworthy and honest agent.

Rabbi Ashlag writes as follows:

> The virtue of each individual within their community is evaluated not according to their own virtue, but the extent to which they serve the whole community. And the opposite — we evaluate the wickedness of each individual only by the degree to which they hurt the whole community, not by their individual, private worth.

(from the essay "HaShalom BaOlam" (Peace in the World)).

Albert Einstein wrote in Why Socialism? *Monthly Review*, May, 1949: I have now reached the point where I may indicate briefly what to me constitutes the essence of the crisis of our time. It concerns the relationship of the individual to society. The individual has become more conscious than ever of his dependence upon society. But he does not experience this dependence as a positive asset, as an organic tie, as a protective force, but rather as a threat to his natural rights, or even to his economic existence…All human beings, whatever their position in society, are suffering from this process of deterioration…prisoners of their own egotism… *Man can find meaning in life, short and perilous as it is, only through* devoting himself to society.

What about Self-Development – is it Devoid of Meaning?

If we exercise, eat healthy foods, pray, practice yoga, learn languages, meditate, put on *tefillin*, take enrichment courses, read literature, spend time pondering solitarily in the forest, are our efforts to improve ourselves devoid of value because others aren't involved?

The answer is that these things are definitely important, even *very important*, but none of them is the goal for which you were sent here. As the Slonimer Rebbe wrote:

> If someone immersed himself in the Torah and the commandments all day, however, if he did not do perform acts of generosity and kindness, that is not considered a day.

("Netivot Shalom" (Paths of Peace))

Put simply: If you're developing spiritually, personality-wise, psychologically, financially, educationally, and in other ways, and that development isn't leading you to change, on the level of your daily life, your attitude toward others, if your development doesn't express itself in actions which impact on others, in kindness and giving, in concern for your brothers and sisters and your country, in concern for all people – then in what significant way *does* it express itself?

Are you developing only in order to focus on yourself, on your needs, on your private desires, and disconnecting from the rest of yourself?

"All sustainable wealth comes from enriching others in some way," the author Brian Tracy wrote.

"I woke up, only to find that the rest of the world is still asleep," wrote Leonardo da Vinci.

> Sometimes it seems to me that people get mixed up. They set up their dream business, invest infinite effort, money, and time in it, and think that they're on a tremendous mission for humanity. What are they busy with? The money that they will make. Money is very important, but is it the goal?

Esty's Spirituality

Esty came to me two weeks after her divorce was finalized. She was already fifty years old, and wanted to clarify, through me, the purpose of her life. It wasn't possible not to ask the obvious question: what caused her divorce?

Esty answered: "We divorced because he didn't understand me. I studied, developed spiritually, and took courses; it's ten years now that I've been improving myself, and he remained the same guy that he was twenty-five years ago."

"It could be," I answered her, "that indeed it would have been difficult to save your marriage, and I'm certainly not going to argue with you about what has already been done, but if I can, I would like to ask you just one question: how was it that the spiritual development you underwent, and the many years long profound study, led you to disconnect from your husband and look down at him? Why didn't your spiritual development lead you to include him, to influence him, or simply to cope with the disparities between you?"

Spiritual development means disconnecting from someone who isn't like me? Should the newly-observant disengage from his secular family, or on the contrary, learn to respect them even more?

This couple was divorced for six years. About half a year ago, she told me that they remarried!

The Main Question

What, then is the main question a person has to deal with?

From what we said here, it seems that the question of purpose is the main question a person has to deal with; there is no more important question.

What kind of person are you?

What are your character traits? What are your values?

Are you a good person, or, God forbid, not good?

All these questions are important, but they're just an expression of the main question, which is: *did you act in the world to fulfill the mission you were sent on*?

Rabbi Ashlag writes:

> I maintain: The first and only mitzvah is… to accept upon oneself to work for your own needs only as much as is absolutely necessary, that is, only enough to maintain your existence. And the rest of the time, you should work for the public, to save the downtrodden, and all the people in the world who need salvation and benefit.

*(The essays "*Mitzvah achat*" (One commandment))*
*("*Pri chacham*" (Fruit of the wise))*

A Dairy Mission

Imagine that you sent your child to a nearby grocery store to buy milk. The child marches to the grocery store, and on the way he meets different people and has exciting experiences. At last he returns, exhilarated, and tells you what happened. It's reasonable to assume that at some point you will ask him, "And where is the milk? What you told us about is all very exciting, and the journey is very important, but the mission – did you do it?"

Now imagine that he throws his hands up, puts them on his head, and says "Oops, I forgot."

I imagine that the moral is clear. I didn't send you to "get excited" (of course we're not talking about the excitement that comes from natural wonders, the rain or the sun, which you're more than invited to get excited about, but in life, we tend to be "moved" by a quite a few unimportant things: he resigned from the government, she won a reality show. Why is it important that I know all of this?)

In the generation of the Internet and readily available information, every word that someone says makes an impression on us, every goal scored in Spain and England, every shirt a celebrity wore in America, all these electrify us, and the result is that we waste the few years granted to us (to perform our mission, of course, what else?) being dazed and drugged by a variety of external toxins/impressions, and by the entertainment which we watch, which scatter and diffuse our consciousness and our spiritual powers.

Our minds, thoughts, feelings have become scattered, *and the question of all questions we have left, orphaned, in a corner: what is our mission?*

We have sold eternity for a fleeting stew of lentils.

The Water Tap and the Hose

So that we can better understand the first insight, which says that "the mission is always directed towards others," we'll liken it to a water tap, a hose, and a garden.

1. The "garden" is the people we are "watering."
2. The hose is you, of course. The agents.
3. The water tap is the power through which we draw the water which you provide to the world, and have impact upon it.

Anything you can think of that a person can do that isn't for others, from sports to personal development, is designed to maintain and improve the hose, that means to say, the person themselves and their abilities, for the sake of others, for their garden.

And taking care of the "hose" (the person themselves) isn't a mission?

It isn't the mission, but it's a great responsibility the hose has, as it says in the Bible "And you will very carefully protect yourselves" (Deuteronomy 4:15). In order that the messengers perform their mission, they surely must eat, sleep at least seven hours every night, and so on.

However, someone's sweet sleep isn't the mission itself; rather, it is designed to maintain the hose so that it can perform its mission.

See how the Ramchal puts it:

> If someone has great wisdom, they are obligated to teach it to anyone who needs it... As the Sages said: "If you have learned much Torah, don't give yourself credit – that's why you were created." If they are rich – they should be happy with what they have, and must help those who are in need; if they are strong – they must help the weak and rescue the oppressed. What is this comparable to? To the household help, every one of whom is in charge of something, and everyone should do their job, to properly take care of the house and its needs.

(*"The Path of the Just,"* **chapter 22**)

Wait, What About Me? Who will Look After My Interests, If All Day I'm Busy Being a Faithful Emissary?

The Sages answered this question with a sharp, on-target statement: Those who pray for their neighbors – their requests for themselves are answered first. This is certainly a strange sentence. What about those who pray for themselves? Aren't they answered?

The Sages answer that **the gates of tears aren't locked**, and if someone reaches a state of desperation, the gate will be opened to their prayer. Apparently, if not, the gates are locked.

Strange. Why does God lock the gates?

Answer: If you're egoistic and concerned only with yourself, you have to know that you're not in the right direction.

The Zohar even describes those who pray only for themselves as "**barking like dogs**." *Hav-hav* is a play on words in the Aramaic, means "give me, give me."

Then what? I shouldn't pray for myself?

That's impossible to say, for prayer itself surely changes and influences you. Therefore, the Sages gently stated the solution: others should pray for you, and you should pray for others.

Elsewhere, the Sages explain the same idea as follows: Messengers for the performance of a mitzvah are not hurt. That is, you should worry about giving to others what they need, and stop worrying about what will happen to you. The One Who has to worry about you will take care of this.

A Soldier in the Reserves or a Relationships Counselor?

A few years ago I was given an urgent call-up for three weeks of reserve duty on a few days' notice. Since I'm busy most of the time with courses and lectures that are set up months in advance, organizing the cancellation of the lectures was really complicated.

On the morning I was to report, it became clear that this was just the beginning: Within one hour, I got telephone calls from three different couples, each one submerged deeply in their own crisis, and all of them had to meet me urgently.

I remember myself walking through the parking lot of my

apartment building, raising my hands heavenward and shouting to the Almighty "I can't cancel my reserve duty myself. If You want me to save these couples' relationships, help me too and get me released from reserve duty, and if I'm needed more in the Reserves, send Your children help from some other source, and I'll make my mark as a soldier."

Answers from God usually don't come instantaneously, as from a magic wand, but they come. About an hour before midnight of that day, in a far-off army base in the Golan, the commander decided that he didn't need all of us, and asked who wanted to be released. Most of the reserves soldiers had already arranged absence from work, and decided to stay. After all, reserve duty is not such a bad distraction from reality…

I and two others decided to be released, and before the commander changed his mind, we left the base and started hitchhiking… I got home at four in the morning, and at 10 the first couple showed up for counseling.

See how Rabbi Kook puts it:

The person must release himself from his private framework, which fills his essence, so that all his thoughts are only directed towards his personal fortune, for this brings the person down to the depths of triviality, and there is no end to the consequent physical and spiritual pain. A person suffers because they take care of themselves instead of their mission; rather, their thoughts and intents and the basis of their ideas must be directed to generality, to the generality of everything, the generality of the world, of humanity, of the Jewish people, of the universe, which is the subject of their mission, not they themselves. And from this, their individuality will also be properly founded.

I remember that in the course of the years when I was in college, before important tests, I would make up a "test" for my fellow students; in that way, by helping others, I internalized the material in the best possible way.

The continuation of Rabbi Kook's words:

> The stronger the general conception is by a person, the more his happiness grows, and the more he merits the divine light…

("Orot Hakodesh" (Lights of Holiness), 3:147)

Have we already mentioned the fact that, in general, those who are conscious of and connected to their mission are the happiest people? The Sages say, "The candle which lights another one loses nothing at all." And therefore, the vacuum is filled, and the filler is just as full as before. Someone who makes others laugh never stops laughing themselves.

It's More Comfortable to be a Private Righteous Person

When we read about Noah in the Book of Genesis he is a righteous man, blameless in his generations, we're filled with appreciation for the dear man who saves the animal world and all of humanity, with the help of the ark that he builds. Our appreciation decreases a little when you read Rashi's comment: **some of our rabbis interpret Noah critically** – if Noah had been in a different generation, for example, in the generation of Avraham, our father, he wouldn't have been considered to be a righteous man at all.

Why? What is our Sages' critique of Noah? The answer is that Noah was a private *tsaddik* (righteous man). One hundred and twenty years pass between the time God announces the flood to Noah, and when the first drop falls.

What did Noah do all this time? He worked on building the ark, and didn't bother at all to pray for all the inhabitants of the world, who were facing annihilation. He didn't try to change their behavior, and he never bothered to argue and bargain with God, as Abraham and Moshe did after him.

What did he do? Build the ark. Therefore, for the Jews, Noah isn't considered "our father," although historically he is. What was he missing? Rabbi Kook writes:

> The more that someone ascends spiritually, the more he feels the great value of the public, the community.

("Orot Hakodesh" (Lights of Holiness) 3: 187)

The goal isn't to go up to the mountain and be alone with God. Maybe for forty days, yes, but after that you have to go down and lead this stiff-necked nation in the desert.

You're Not the Subject

I often find myself unable to understand messengers who are, forgive me, too busy with themselves. Listen, I say, with all due respect, you're not the subject here. People need you, and as long as you're preoccupied with your fears and uncertainties, then your garden is withering. Who will water it?

So in the next chapter, we will take responsibility for your fears, so that you can finally free yourself from them.

Summary of the First Insight:

"The Mission is Always Directed Towards Others":

- If we're all part of society, a location, and if we're all maintained by one other; if we're all like one body with different organs, then everything is connected to everything. Nothing is detached, independent, unrelated to the whole.
- The understanding that our mission is always directed towards others should help us point the arrow outwards and ask: What can I give *them*? Or, what do *they* need from *me*?
- A person doesn't correct himself directly, but rather by changing his attitude toward others.
- There are many coaches/mentors/businessmen/celebrities that write books and give lecturers that say that if you take these or those steps, you will get rich; they portray wealth as the purpose of life. This, however, is not the case. You didn't come here to get rich; you came to enrich.
- You are, sir, aren't the subject. You, madam, aren't the subject. The mission is always directed towards others.
- Do you want to complete the first insight from another viewpoint, that of neuroscience? Watch this TED lecture on YouTube: Jill Bolt Taylor: My stroke of insight.

Exercise for the First Insight – "The Genie in the Bottle"

You're strolling down the street and you see an oil lamp covered with dust. You pick it up and rub it. Suddenly, a genie comes out and says, "Your wish is my command. I grant you three wishes. But be aware: you can't ask for anything for others, just for yourselves."

"Also, you can't ask for a wish that I can't perform, such as, for example, 'make me happy.'"

The wishes:

1. _____
   _____
   _____

2. _____
   _____
   _____

3. _____
   _____
   _____

Please note: I want to grant you another wish, but its rules are different. I want you to ask for a wish for others who need something. If you had all the time, skills, and money in the world, what would you ask for and give them?

Explanation:

Some people are materially needy, that is to say, they don't have anything to eat or they don't have anywhere to live, and so on.

Some people are medically needy; they need a doctor's care, or a massage, and so on.

Some people need education; they need to be taught.

Some people need an emotional conversation, a process, a listening ear, emotional help.

Some people need spirituality, religiosity, and ritualism.

Some need good advice or help in moments of crisis.

Some people need a medical clown to cheer them up.

Some need someone to go along with them during a weight-loss process.

There are children at risk, there are children who come from difficult families, there are children with objective problems.

Some people need to find a spouse.

There are battered women; there are lonely Holocaust survivors.

And this is only a partial list. Maybe something else bothers you, and you want to change and improve things?

Please think: If you had everything you need: time, money, means, human resources, personal ability, whom from among all those in need would you help?

To pinpoint the question: if, for example, it pains you that there are children hungry for bread, but it also pains you, but less so, that there are also parents who can't manage the family budget as they should, would you build a system that would make charitable donations flow towards them, or would you sit with them on managing the family budget so that their being needy could be prevented?

The fourth wish is: **I would like to help in the area of**

_____

It's hard for me to see distress in _____, and I would like to change things.

It's important to me to help in the above area because:

1. _____

   _____

   _____

2. _____

   _____

   _____

3. _____

   _____

   _____

If in the course of finding your calling you find that your desire to help is connected to some personal failure, you should know that there are signs here that can't be ignored.

This Insight Wouldn't be Complete Without the Following Story:

The story is told about a father and son who came before Rabbi Aryeh Levin, arguing angrily about the only coat at their disposal. The son said, I go out to work in the cold and rain, and my father stays home. He should give me the coat.

The father said: I am old and my son is young. I need the coat, he can manage without it; when I was his age, I managed without a coat.

Rabbi Levine looked at them and sent them home with a request that they return the next day. When they returned, the rabbi asked them to make each other's claims. Then the son said: My father is an old man, I am young, I can manage, the coat definitely must stay with him. The father said: I'm at home, I can cover myself with something else; it's better that my son, who goes out in the cold and the rain, take the coat.

When they were done, Rabbi Aryeh Levin removed a coat from his closet and handed it to the stunned father and son. Take it, he told them, I don't need it. Just before leaving his home, they asked him: Your Honor, why did you make us come back today? Why couldn't you have given us this coat when we were here yesterday?

"Yesterday, when you were here," he answered them, "everyone said '*my* coat,' so I too said '*my* coat, it's *mine*.' But today, when everyone was ready to hand the coat over to someone else, I also was ready to hand my coat over to others."

SECOND INSIGHT

NO ONE WILL PERFORM YOUR MISSION FOR YOU

And no, not all people are equal... and no man will be able to do what his friend does. This must be thoroughly understood.

(Rabbi Yitzchak Luria, the Ari, *Mavo Shearim* **2:3:9)**

I don't want to start with an insubordinate question, but isn't it possible that people may be doing everything in their power to evade their mission?

People tend to think: There are enough therapists/teachers/doctors/bankers and more, right? What do they need me as well for? I'll continue to be afraid of my own shadow, I'll continue to do what people tell me to do, nothing more, so that they won't pay any attention to me and tell me that I'm worth something, or, God forbid, that I have some talent, and by mistake even appoint me to a responsible position.

It may sound strange, but most people run away from their dreams, fearing to go the limit with their skills.

Really? You prefer **not** *to be yourselves* rather than to be your-selves? Isn't that a recipe for an unending sense of bitterness?

Surely, your answer will be, don't worry about us, we will

silence our depression and bitterness with TV/junk food/ cigarettes/ anti-depressants/shopping/ drugs.

I'm sorry to say that I must inform you that you aren't alone. Most people prefer to work for someone else's dream, not to ask tough questions, not to confront themselves, not to admit that there's a mission that's very obligating, and demands commitment.

> We must also censure the smallness of people's faith in themselves, their lack of recognition of the virtue of their soul, in order for them to return to their proper size.
>
> *(Rabbi Kook, "Shmona Kvatzim" (Eight Collections), 3:196)*

Don't worry, you're not the only one who avoiding their mission, knowingly or unconsciously. People as great as Jonah the prophet ran away too. Jonah the prophet, as well as Moshe Rabbeinu, the great leader of the people of Israel, tried to evade their lives' missions, even though they knew deeply that the "factor" that laid the mission on them is a "tough character" from whom it's hard to run away.

Moshe tried to shirk his mission using five arguments, among other things, on the grounds that he was a tongue-tied stutterer.

He was right. It's hard to be a stuttering leader.

But he also used the following argument:

> And Moses said to God, *Who am I*, that I should go to Pharaoh, and that I should take the children of Israel out of Egypt?
>
> *(Exodus 3:11)*

Who am I? I know that phrase from somewhere. Honestly, I'm sick of hearing these words. I hear them every day from people blessed with loads of talent.

The question arises: was it impossible to transfer the task to someone else, instead of Moses?

God gives Jonah a mission, to convey a message to the people of Nineveh. What does Jonah do? And Jonah arose to flee to Tarshish, away from the presence of the Lord.

From Whose presence? We're always running away from Him and His missions.

And he went down to Jaffa and found a ship going to Tarshish, and he paid his fare, and he went aboard to go with them to Tarshish, away from the presence of the Lord. And the Lord cast a great wind into the sea (in case you thought He would give up).

And there was a great storm in the sea, and the ship was likely to be wrecked, and the sailors were afraid, and each man cried out to his god. And they threw the cargo that was in the ship into the sea, to make it lighter; and Jonah went down into the bowels of the ship, and laid down and fell asleep. What are you sleeping for, Jonah?

The captain came to him, and said to him: 'Why are you sleeping? Get up, call upon your God; maybe He will think of us, and we will not perish.' And the sailors said to one another: 'Come, let's cast lots, so that we may know who caused this evil to befall us.' So they cast lots, and the lot fell upon Jonah. Then they said to him: 'Tell us, please, what caused this evil to befall us: what is your occupation, where do you come from? What is your country, and who are your people?'

(Jonah 1:3)

You're not by chance part of the "Chosen People," are you? Because if you are, we're in deep trouble.

> And he said unto them, 'I am a Jew, and I fear the Lord, the God of heaven, who made the sea and the land.'
>
> And the men were very afraid, and said unto him, 'What have you done?' For they knew he was running away from the Lord, because he told them.
>
> *(Jonah 1:9)*

Don't you realize by now that private and public troubles come because people run away from their mission?

> And they said unto him, 'What should we do to you that the sea become calm for us?' for the sea was becoming even stormier. And he said 'Pick me up and throw me into the sea, and the sea will become calm for you, for I know that this great storm happened to you because of me.'
>
> *(Jonah 1:12-15)*

Is that the solution? So that you don't suffer because I don't fulfill my mission, it's better to get rid of me? Throw me into the sea? Jonah the prophet was completely confused.

Of course Jonah has no choice, and eventually, he does fulfill his mission.

Is Jonah irreplaceable?

And the question remains. Is it impossible without Jonah?

If Jonah is afraid of the mission and runs away from it, is it impossible to send another volunteer to Nineveh? Can't salvation come from somewhere else?

The answer is that yes, you can send another messenger instead. It isn't ideal, but if you don't do your job, salvation will come from somewhere else.

This is what is written in the Book of Esther:

> For if you are completely silent now, the Jews' salvation will come from somewhere else.

Mordechai says this key phrase to Esther, but not only to her.

This sentence is like an echo which reverberates to us as if to say, you have — as individuals and as a nation — a mission. It is as if the Higher Power says: I gave you the opportunity to be My partner, to help Me to uncover in reality the love and the good I prepared for you, but if you decline — I'll manage alone. I don't need you exclusively, I can turn the poor into non-poor in a minute, but I'm making it possible for *you* to do it.

Why? Because reality is created so that you will be My partners, so that you yourselves can grow. What independent value do you have if Mommy and Daddy do everything themselves? How will the children grow up and experience "being grown up" unless their father and mother allow them to participate and take part?

This is exactly what the *Midrash* says. God isn't looking for robots or "small children" who do what they are told. God seeks partners:

> From the beginning of the creation of the world, the Almighty wished to enter into a *partnership* with our material world.

*("Yalkut Shimoni," **Genesis – Chapter 1 — Remez 5**)*

In the end, despite the danger, Esther did her job, made her commitment, and this is one of the reasons that the biblical book is named after her and not after Mordechai.

So, Do I or Don't I Have a Replacement?

One of the most prominent messages people receive during their lives, especially at work, is that "everyone has a substitute." That message, with regards to the functioning of the organization, is usually correct, but is it true as a general observation - to a person's functioning in reality?

On the contrary. You don't have a substitute. If you could do "copy/paste," if Tzila were an *exact* copy of Gila, then one of them wouldn't exist. As the Baal Shem Tov said:

> the day you were born is the day the Almighty decided that the world can't exist without you.

It seems to me that there is no perception that strengthens, empowers, cultivates, and maintains sanity, like this very thought. It's impossible for the world to function without me, without my part in this enormous jigsaw puzzle. This is a sentence that places responsibility on your shoulders on the one hand, and great, empowering comfort on the other hand.

> The greatness of the Holy One, blessed be He, is, that when a man molds coins with one press, each of them is exactly like all the others, but the King of Kings, the Holy One, blessed be He, *has molded all people with the seal of Adam, and no one of them exactly resembles anyone else.*

(Sanhedrin 4: 5)

Just as, according to Jewish law, *even one letter missing in the Torah scroll makes it invalid,* so too, our world needs every part, including me, for if it didn't need me, I wouldn't have been created.

Rabbi Samson Raphael Hirsch writes:

> God needs in His world's economy the moss and the cedar, the stalk and the vine. Everything received its own unique portion, and is happy with it and fulfills His commandment. The moss does not envy the cedar, and the stalk does not envy the vine. The vine will not ask to be a stalk, and cedar will not aspire to be moss. They put the world's plan in God's hands, and are happy and content to contribute, in the kingdom of His world, their contribution to the whole.

(Genesis 1: 11)

Hence, my very existence is a testament to my necessity. Precisely now, precisely in this generation, specifically to these parents.

Rabbi Ashlag writes:

> Know that these (the person's unique powers, which it's forbidden to harm or change) are the true possessions of the individual... Thus, anyone who destroys some kind of tendency of the individual, and uproots it from them, causes the world to lose that lofty and wonderful conception... because that tendency will never happen again, in any other body but theirs.

("HaCherut" (Freedom))

And look how Rabbi Shlomo Wolbe expresses it:

Everyone is a one-time creation. And every human being must know: I, with my powers and qualities, my countenance and my spiritual qualities, am unique in the world among all those who live now — no one is like me now, no one was like me in past generations, and no one will be like me in the future, until the end of the generations. If so, God must have sent me to the world on a special mission which no one else can fulfill; only I, in my once-ness, can.

("Alei Shur")

Sounds simple and positive, and who won't agree with this? However, in practice, when a person meets their mission, they will also meet their greatest fears, their insecurity. Fears don't arise when a person has to implement just his minor talents/skills.

If, for example, Hagit's dream is to work with "youth in distress" and she is undecided whether this is her mission or not, she will usually be afraid, and it will seem "too much for her." Really, Hagit? Too much for you?

Usually, the reason is that with Hagit, as in most of us, self-confidence is "result-dependent" — if I succeed that's an indication that I'm "worth something," and if I don't, then it seems I'm not. So she thinks it's "too much for her," in order to avoid failure. Her greatness frightens her.

This book tries to remove this lie from your mind and your heart. You're much more special, important and of worth, whether you succeed or you fail, You yourselves, independent of one outcome or another — you're a special "illumination," unparalleled in the world.

Fear

It's difficult to criticize a person who is afraid. It's a natural emotion; it's not just natural, but it's also positive in certain aspects. Caution, for example, is a very positive result of fear. Reverence is also a positive consequence. Those who have no fear at all are unbalanced.

But what if fear crosses the line, causing terror and dread for no rational reason? Look what Rav Kook writes about it:

> Excessive fear takes the splendor of life out of man... There is nothing as wrong and cruel in the world. It infinitely magnifies all evils, and darkens the glow of all good things... showing that evil is hidden somewhere, rather than the obvious good.

Every little risk turns into a monster in the eyes of those who are too afraid, and all good disappears:

Fearful people ask themselves:

And if that does not work?

And if I cannot make a living from what I love most doing?

How can I live up to the standards of others?

And what if I myself am not satisfied with the product? How can I sell it to someone else?

And what if I can't keep up with the timetable they demand of me?

And what if they ask me to do something I'm not good at?

Rav Kook continues:

> The source of all moral, intellectual and material weakness is unrestrained fear, and that alone. Fear threatens the person not to do anything to save themselves, not to lift a finger to rescue themselves, lest they be harmed,

lest they bring unforgivable evil upon themselves, until it makes the person weak and feeble, until, through laziness and immobility, the person is tripped up by anything that is evil.

People try to "go for a sure thing." Not to stand out, not to take risks, and from that, ultimately, comes sadness, laziness, immobility, and bitterness.

And wonder of wonders, Rav Kook goes on to say that not only are a person's fears unrealistic, and are mainly imagined, but the more talented one is, the greater their fears are:

The most harmful fear is the intellectual fear, which *delusion* casts on the finest and most magnificent part of the human race...*and the more the ability of a person to understand and to learn grows, the greater his imaginary fear is*, through the activity of the mind.

(Eder Hayakar, "Fear")

So what should we do?

Did you notice that Rabbi Kook used the term "delusion?"

We will look for our delusions and change them.

That is, *fear is an emotion whose source is thoug*ht — if you change the false thoughts or the false fantasies — the emotion will also change. If you think like King David, who said "Even when I walk in the valley of the shadow of death, I will fear no evil, for You are with me" — where will fear come from?

So here are some common delusions that I come across again and again while working with people on their mission:

Delusion #1: I Am Not Deserving

Perhaps my answer will surprise you, but when someone makes a statement about himself like: "Who says I really deserve to be a relationship counselor? Who says I really deserve to be a doula? There are doulas with more experience than me, and marriage counselors with thirty years' experience," I usually answer: *Right. You, sir, really are not deserving. You, madam, really are not deserving.*

What makes you worthy? University studies? Specialization? Experience? I know "experts" who can put a check mark next to any possible qualification on their own resume, and yet have made, and are still making, serious mistakes.

You and I *are not deserving*, but if so, who is deserving? The answer is that *the person who needs you* is the one who deserves you. Or it's more precise to say it this way: although you're not perfect – you're worthy of helping them, of giving them of your uniqueness.

Of all the consultants in the world, they came to you. Therefore, if you're aware of a different "messenger" who in this case can help more, be honest with the person who came to you and tell them your opinion; be specific and explain why they should go to someone else. But if not — give of yourself. Be the best "hose" you can be for them.

After all, of all the doulas in the world, she turned specifically to you.

Rabbi Yehuda Ashlag, a 20th-century Kabbalist who translated, interpreted and explained the holy Zohar and the writings of the Ari of blessed memory, writes at the end of his days as follows:

And who knows as well as I do that *I don't deserve* at all even to be just a messenger and a scribe to reveal secrets like these, and there is no need to say to understand them at their roots. And why did God do this to me? Only because the generation deserves it.

("Shofro shel Mashiach" (the Messiah's Ram's Horn))

In other words, Rabbi Ashlag says: it wasn't because of my great wisdom and not because of my righteousness, but since the generation needs this mission — I was chosen.

And there are also messengers from the other side of the divide, *who think the public doesn't deserve them* (there are also some of these, unfortunately) and that is their excuse not to fulfill their mission.

Usually, I refer them to the following quotation that appears in the book *"Orchot Tzadikim"*:

The wise man says: "Do kindness with those who deserve it, and those who do not deserve it — you will be worthy of doing it."

("Shaar Hanedivut" (The Gate of Generosity)

Here is the place to share my own delusion with you: There are quite a few people who asked me why I don't train trainers. "We think," they said, after personally experiencing my unique technique, "there's a need to duplicate you."

So my answer to everyone was: "It's too soon, *I'm not worthy yet* to train others, as I'm too young and don't have enough experience."

Delusion #2: It Must Be Perfect

Perfectionism is a good trait that helps a person to be precise, to pay attention to details, to extract the best from themselves and not compromise on mediocrity. The problem is that sometimes perfectionism exceeds its limits, and striving for perfection makes the person get stuck, and ultimately causes paralysis and inaction. You have no idea how many people don't expose themselves to the light, don't let their dreams go free, because of perfectionism. If I were a perfectionist, I would not have published five books. All of them have a lot of flaws. All of them are imperfect. So why did I nevertheless publish an imperfect product?

1. Because I'm not God. All in all, I'm just a human being.
2. For even God creates imperfect creations which need correction.
3. Because the generation needs these books, and if I aspire to perfection, then they will remain in a drawer.
4. They can always be fixed in the next edition. In the next lecture.
5. Because I understood that, during the course of life, first of all, do something, and only then improve it while still in motion. Otherwise, you get stuck.

So what do you suggest to me if I'm a perfectionist who is failing to make progress?

Perfectionism comes from conditional love. People who aspire to perfection grew up in an atmosphere in which they were judged and criticized constantly. Their basic experience was that they're not good enough, not "okay" enough, they don't meet expectations.

The solution is unconditional love. Since we can't go back to childhood, we ask ourselves – from whom can I get unconditional love? "From myself" is one challenging answer, but usually we don't give ourselves this gift. "From God" is another answer, for those who believe. From my spouse/my children, etc.

Delusion #3: It's Immodest Possibly Even Arrogant, to Call Myself a Messenger

You don't say. Does the story of Jonah escaping to the ship and the claims of Moshe in the presence of the bush testify to humility? In my opinion, yes. It's humility — a very specific kind of humility called "false humility." One might mistakenly think that we're talking about Jonah's and Moses' praiseworthy humility, but what we have here isn't proper humility, but rather false humility.

God informed both of them of their error so that they could correct it. People who are believed in, who are given abilities and support, to whom plenty is sent, and who nevertheless don't realize their potential and the skills that they merited receiving, are not called humble; they're called fools, fools who throw away what they were given.

All this manifests itself not only in regard to others, but also in regard to ourselves, in our inner conversation with ourselves. Most people whom I know do a lot for others, but they mistakenly call it "livelihood" or "work," and thus they take all the air out of their own sails, they renounce all that can give their lives content, a reason to get up in the morning. They turn the means — money — into a goal. Money is a goal? Those easily-disappearing bills covering the bank overdraft, which only live for a moment — they are a goal?

Meaningfulness? Mission? These words are too lofty for too many messengers.

They tell me, "Come on, what matters is that we can make

a decent living."

The time has come to put the word "mission" on the table (a word that incidentally in Hebrew is derived from the word messenger…) and look it straight in the eyes. *"Mission" isn't a dirty word, and it certainly isn't arrogance.*

Please set aside the invalid, social humility that makes people descend to the lowest common denominator, to engage only in barely surviving and making it through the month.

Here's a suggestion: Want to be humble? Save all matters of humility for after your daily mission has been completed.

Then, when you confront yourselves every night before you go to sleep, you're all welcome to say that all that you have done, everything that you've taken care of and everyone you helped, isn't yours, that a hidden hand blessed you with strength and skill, made others like you, and gave you the power of speech and the energy to act.

Or in the words of Hillel the Sage, in Pirkei Avot (the Ethics of the Fathers):

When you wake up in the morning, say: If I am not (here) for myself, (then) who am I(here for)?

That looks like a sentence which is the opposite of humility, but actually is the epitome of humility, for if we don't get up and act — who will?

Who will help couples in crisis? Who will treat patients? Who will open the kindergarten and grant their warmth and wisdom to thirty little children?

Rav Kook writes:

One must be more afraid of lowliness than of exaltedness.

That is, we have greater need to avoid the false humility that usually causes a person to diminish themselves, and as a result to be weak and sad, than we need to avoid the pride that helps a person to act in the world.

Anyone who says "Who am I that I should..." seems to be humble, but the truth is that this is arrogance, because they're so busy with themselves and whether they're talented enough and good enough, that ultimately the plants in their garden, which they and only they should be watering — wither.

Continuation of the advice: As you go to sleep, please read the rest of Hillel's words:

And me, just by myself, what am I?

Without the blessings and gifts of the Almighty, without the education and love that I received from my parents, without all the tools my good environment gave me, without all my failures, without the Torah that illuminates my path — what am I? As it's written in Deuteronomy Chapter 8:

Remember the Lord your God — for He gives you the strength to achieve.

The passage in *Pirkei Avot* concludes:

And if not now when?

With all the goodness in you, your life experience, all the knowledge you have accumulated, *with all your ability to benefit others — if you don't do good now, today and every single minute — when will you?*

It seems to me that the one who focuses a spotlight most accurately on the delusion I mentioned here is Marianne

Williamson, an American writer who was quoted in the past by Nelson Mandela in one of his speeches:

> Our deepest fear is not that we are inadequate. Our deepest fear is that we are powerful beyond measure. It is our light, not our darkness, that most frightens us… You are a child of God. Playing small does not serve the world. *There is nothing enlightened about shrinking* so that other people won't feel insecure around you… We were born to make manifest the glory of God that is within us. It's not just in some of us; it's in everyone.

Delusion #4: The Attitude Toward Money

The truth is that your mission doesn't have to be part of your livelihood. You can, of course, volunteer, but here we will deal with the case in which your mission is also your livelihood; there is no reason in the world that it shouldn't be.

I sit and listen to so many talented, good, tremendously giving people, who repeat over and over the following sentences:

But why should they pay me for something I like to do?

Why should I make a living from what comes to me easily?

It's so hard for me to demand money for the service I give.

I don't know how aware you are of this problem, but most people are sure that only a few people make a living from what they love to do, and all the rest suffer in order to make a living from a job they don't like but must work at. There are no words to describe how defeatist this approach is.

I have a friend, an artist by trade. I have never understood what people find in his paintings; I have never understood how he supported a family from his mediocre paintings.

It turns out that there are several prestigious galleries that don't agree with me, and he is flooded with orders and people pay large sums for his work.

When Boaz, a relationships therapist, shared with his wife his intention to change his method in his meetings with couples, and that he intends to start therapy by holding a deep and meaningful four-hour session with them and charging them $500, she was horrified: "Why would someone pay you such a sum?" she asked "That's a lot!"

It could be that she's right, but in practice, Boaz's diary is flooded with appointments.

The truth is that there is no reason in the world that anyone whom you help, who makes use of your skills, shouldn't pay you the amount that you set as a fee. You're justified in charging money for service, consultation, or work.

You think that you don't deserve money for your work or for your efforts, because it "comes to you easily?" Why not? So what?

A lawyer deserves to be paid $1000 for signing a document?

A masseuse deserves to be paid $150 for a 45-minute massage?

Please look at these simple facts:

1. You didn't steal this money; you worked for it.
2. The other person has agreed to pay you the amount you asked for.
3. What will you do with the money you earned honestly? Buy drugs? How can anyone who has small children to feed in his home be ashamed to take money? And even someone who doesn't have little mouths to feed but gives "added value" to another person, perhaps thereby even changing their life — why should they be ashamed to

charge a fee for it?

4. The other person benefits from paying you, because they're left with the feeling that they're not "freeloaders," but have paid you for your efforts.

5. The government will benefit from the taxes you pay, and the economy will flourish.

6. The money puts the relationship between the giver and the recipient into a clear, professional and well-understood framework.

7. A person who charges a reasonable fee for their work is usually highly regarded, and those who demand a smaller sum are, in most cases, treated with contempt.

Delusion #5: The Mission is Limited to Only One Place

Our mission is everywhere, literally at any moment.

A few years ago, Eyal, someone in his late thirties, sat before me, wanting to clarify his purpose. He had a business importing medical products for laboratories. He got into the import field by chance because he lived abroad for several years as a young man. Being an importer wasn't even close to his dreams, so he was frustrated. On the one hand, he wanted to make a breakthrough; on the other hand, he was committed to supporting his family. We tried for four hours to zero in on his skills from every angle. We talked about dreams, about desires, about childhood fantasies, but we couldn't come to a clear-cut conclusion. Sometimes it takes time.

Eyal, on the other hand, actually did come to a conclusion: I'm a nothing, I don't seem to have a mission in this world (it's so easy to give up.)

We ordered another coffee and I asked him to tell me about the people who needed him in everyday life. Of course his wife and children were at the top of the list, the employees he employed and to whom he provided a livelihood also got into the conversation, his sick mother was mentioned, and finally, we even got to the synagogue, to which he actually doesn't go regularly. However, he once chanced to come to a service in which they suddenly asked "Is there a *Kohen* (Jewish priest) here among the worshipers?" and his hand was raised, the only one in the in large synagogue (*Kohanim*, Jewish priests, bless the people in the course of the service, and thus they fulfill a mission). That morning, Eyal blessed about 50 religious worshipers, although he himself is far from religious practice.

Amazing, I told him, even someone who isn't aware of one central mission performs dozens of missions. At any moment, reality may present them with another mission. One time it's in the synagogue and another time — they can save a person's life by advice, help, and so forth.

I gave him an assignment to concentrate on these secondary missions, and we set up a meeting for a month later.

Eyal came back to me really glowing. He felt that even in areas he didn't think about, like in business, for example, his integrity and the way he behaves is really a mission, and people tell him about it, saying how wonderful it is that there are people who can be trusted in today's business world.

We came to the conclusion that right now, even if Eyal has one central mission, he is probably not at the stage to find it yet, and instead, he should concentrate on projecting goodness, being a spotlight of illumination wherever he is. Who knows? Either this itself is his purpose, or the happiness and fulfillment he experiences in the place where he already is will lead him to discover his one central mission.

If so, then let's say this: Isn't motherhood an enormous

mission in itself? Isn't a benevolent expression? Kindness? Helping others? Good advice? Being a full-time grandma?

You don't have to look for exciting, impressive mission descriptions; you can be huge messengers and see missions all over the place.

Delusion #6: It's Better to Work at What is Available and Secure

In the 1980's, the Soviet Union was in severe economic crisis. Long lines lined the streets for loaves of bread. There's a story about a man in Moscow who, while walking, suddenly stopped and bent down for a moment to tie his shoelaces, and immediately stood up. As he stood there, another person then came and stood behind him, then another behind him, and another, until it wasn't long before hundreds of people were standing in line behind the first one, waiting their turn to get something.

At one point, the last man in line asked the man in front of him:

"What are they giving out?"

"I don't know, I'll ask."

So the question went forward through all the people in line, and no one knew what they were waiting for and what they were giving out. When the second man in line asked the first one, he replied, "They're not giving out anything, I just stood still for a moment to tie my shoelaces."

"So why do you keep standing here, and we're standing behind you like fools, if they're not giving out anything here?"

The first man answered him: "I finally got lucky, and for the first time in my life I'm the first in line – you think I should give up my place in line and just go away?"

I remember this story every time someone sits in front of

me and makes excuses why they work in a safe, secure job they don't like, instead of totally following their dreams. From this point of view, standing first in line is always preferable, even if nothing is being given out there.

People who are preoccupied with security, rather than mission and purpose, are generally motivated by fear, by the existential survival struggle that they themselves invited into their lives.

So this is the truth: there can never be a blessing in any work that your heart isn't in, and you won't convince me otherwise by citing the money you earn that finances your superfluous luxuries, or the job's great working conditions.

This delusion will shatter at some point, unless a person decides that they have a job and they have a mission, and they're unconnected, in different areas, and that their mission will manifest itself completely separately from their job. That person gets their happiness from another area they invest in, after working hours.

Or as a bank employee once said to me: "The hours I invest in the bank are for the economic security of my family, and for the peace of mind that allows me to spend my free time playing the clarinet I love so much. And it's not only me — neighbors and friends come to hear me play, and they enjoy themselves. I don't make a living from this, but the soul is delighted, my own and that of others."

Delusion #7 — Tomorrow I'll Have Time — Not Now

There's a story about a journalist who interviewed a terminal patient and asked him, "How is it to get up every morning knowing you're dying very slowly?" The patient replied, "And how is it to get up every morning pretending that you are not?"

If we were to grasp how much sentences like "there is time" and "tomorrow" are delusions, we would throw them into the garbage can. If we would really realize that a moment that passes doesn't come back, we would run to fulfill our dreams and carry out our mission.

A Chinese proverb says: the best time to plant a tree passed twenty years ago. The next best time is — now.

Now is the time to dare, to gather up the courage, to try, to look with open eyes at the reasons which made you keep so much of your cheese. Later, it will spoil.

So far, we've listed widespread delusions. If you have original delusions I didn't mention, I'd love you to share them with me.

We conclude with two tips:

A. Do you want to escape the fear and the delusions? Do you want to stop fearing to carry things out? You won't believe what Rabbi Kook's advice is: be a *chutzpan* – a brazen, audacious person.

> The beginning of all the preparations for the end of days is the removal of thought's excess fear from the general psyche, especially from the souls of the outstanding individuals, those blessed with good intelligence, who are equipped for holiness and justice. This removal is driven by the force which is the opposite of fear — audacity, must be strengthened at this time, for where audacity reveals itself, there is no fear, even though audacity itself comes from a low place.

(Eder Hayakar)Handsome price), **"Fear"**

Rabbi Kook says that *chutzpah*, audacity, isn't a positive trait, but it helps to overcome fear.

To be brazen means to act, to do, to influence, to dare, even when you're not the most talented person in the world, and even if in the beginning the mission is partial and incomplete, even if you make mistakes.

In other words, the fears that we listed above take hold of you *as long as you don't do anything. When you are active, they disappear.*

B. Stop comparing!

How can a zebra be compared to a giraffe? Which is better, a nectarine or a clementine? Deep inside yourself, you know that most of the fears stem from the fact that you're comparing yourself to others.

Summary of the Second Insight:

"No One Else Will Do Your Job for You":

- The whole world is a very narrow bridge, and the main thing is not to scare yourself at all. *(Rabbi Nachman of Breslov, Likutei Moharan (Rav Nachman's Collection))* Note that Rabbi Nachman was being precise when he wrote: "not to scare yourself." That is, fearful people are those who frighten themselves with imaginary fears.
- People are afraid to stand in front of the mirror and say "I was sent here to help youth in distress." Why? Because it's a very big responsibility to confront your mission.
- We all carry out one mission or another everywhere, including those who have not found their main mission.
- The question "Do I deserve it or not" isn't the correct question; rather, the question is: "Who needs me? Whom should I help?"
- People are afraid to turn their vocation into a source of livelihood — why? You're allowed to make money from your mission. It's wrong to separate your mission from earning a living. You're allowed to make money from things that come to you easily.
- There is good, balanced fear called caution or reverence, but excessive fear destroys the life of people.
- A person who is eager to fulfill his mission must develop the quality of *chutzpah*, brazenness or audacity.
- Anyone who runs away from their mission suffers, and they cause all of us to suffer too. Just ask Jonah.
- It's time to stop comparing.

Exercise for the second insight: Relax

Who is willing to volunteer to jump into a burning building to save a cat?

Who is ready, provided that they have a fire-protective suit and a mask with oxygen cylinders, and all the firefighters are there to help them?

When people "get out of the box" and think big, fears and resistance usually wake up. The "stabilizer," people's need for stability, tries to restore balance. So the best exercise, in my opinion, after we dealt with all the above fears that pop up, is to calm people down.

So, what will calm your fears?

What will give you a sense of a "safety net" which will help you to move confidently towards the mission?

Let's think together about what may bother you/arouse resistance/prevent you from marching towards your mission.

For any such resistance — we will provide a "tranquilizer."

Examples:

If what bothers and hinders me are financial worries, then I'll write down the amount I need to get ahead. If I don't have the needed amount, then I won't proceed. A mission isn't suicide.

If I'm concerned that I haven't studied the field in which I want to be active enough — I'll write that I'll engage in my mission only after I study this course or other, etc.

If I'm not ready for battles with my wife, then the tranquilizer will be: I'll do things only with her consent and support, which means that I'll also provide her with "tranquilizers."

If I'm afraid I won't get enough customers for the jewelry workshop I dream of opening, then I'll write a condition that I'll open the workshop only when such and such a number of people register.

If I'm bothered by the time I don't have — I'll record the time that I can devote to the subject, and that's all the time that I will obligate myself to spend on it.

In short, this exercise should reassure us.

The more obstacles/fears/objections we record, and next to each of them its solution/reassuring condition, the less we will resist the idea of the mission:

My Goal/ Mission (which at present may seem "too big for me"): _____

_____

_____

_____

_____

Fear/Conflict/Obstacle #1: _____

_____

_____

_____

A solution for obstacle #1: _____

_____

_____

_____

Fear/Conflict/Obstacle #2:_____

_____

_____

_____

A solution for obstacle #2: _____

_____

_____

_____

Fear/Conflict/Obstacle #3: _____

_____

_____

_____

A solution for obstacle #3: _____

_____

_____

_____

Fear/Conflict/Obstacle #4: _____

_____

_____

_____

A solution for obstacle #4: _____

_____

_____

_____

Fear/Conflict/Obstacle #5: _____

_____

_____

_____

A solution for obstacle #5: _____

_____

_____

_____

Fear/Conflict/Obstacle #6: _____

_____

_____

_____

A solution for obstacle #6: _____

_____

_____

_____

This Insight isn't complete Without the Following Article:
Six Months to Live by Yair Lapid (published in Yediot Aharonot)

What would you do if they told you that you had only six months left to live?

I asked a few friends this question one evening. First everyone gave it some thought, then they started answering.

The lawyer would go to South America. One journalist would write the book that has been sitting, undigested, in his stomach; the other journalist was going to look for his girlfriend from eleventh grade.

Someone talked about the paintings she painted when she was sixteen. To this day, she believes there was something in them, and she wants to check this out. Two said they would stick as close to the children as possible — suck them in, until the end of love. I was undecided between London and three rounds of professional boxing. That conversation was, of course, a little infantile, and a bit too romantic, but only after they left did I understand what was so puzzling:

Why not now? After all, all these dreams were within the realm of possibility. You can try to create all the books and paintings you want after nine in the evening. A plane ride will get you to your old love. And for a few hundred dollars, London is definitely reachable. And even if he does have to sacrifice for this, why shouldn't thirty-four-year-old lawyer not travel to South America for half a year?

Why do we give up so fast? Why do we finalize our daily existence so soon, and close the door and lock ourselves in with it?

So soon we say "mortgage," or "my boss?" Why are most people afraid to get what they really want? And who told them that they can't?

In the past fifteen years, I've spent much of my time interviewing people who "did it." From Bill Gates through Benjamin Netanyahu to Zvika Hadar. There are a few questions that one way or another I asked everyone:

"Why just you? How did it happen? What did you do differently than others?" The answer is that there is no answer.

There are really no qualities that characterize all successful people, except one: they did the irrational thing. Because the real logic is only in mediocrity, in doing what other people are doing, in waiting until the doctor comes in and informs you that you have only six months left to live. And then, sorry, it's already too late.

THIRD INSIGHT

YOUR TALENTS HINT AT YOUR MISSION

The saddest thing in the world is wasted talent.

Chaz Flamintry, *A Bronx Story*

It's time to talk about talent: Every person, and I emphasize, *every person*, has at least one thing that is unique to them, that they are really talented in, that relative to others they excel in. It could be that the talent refers to how they speak, it could be how they sing or paint, it could be that her talent is her motherhood and that his talent is his fatherhood. There is no one who isn't talented, who hasn't received a divine gift of some kind.

Moreover, we have talents which we aren't even aware of. It's likely that we've never been required to use them, or that we weren't raised in a social environment that valued or appreciated them. For example, my wife, who grew up on a kibbutz, used to ride horses all the time, and enjoyed riding very much. I rode on a horse maybe once. My social environment didn't really push people in that direction.

So maybe we should experiment with everything the world

has to offer before we decide what we're good at?

The answer is that you don't have to. Within the talents you are aware of, all the rest are concealed. All your talents create in you *a special tapestry that no one has in the world but you.*

I'm Special?

Am I really special, or is it just convenient to think so? Is there really "no one else like me," or is it only my mother who thinks so?

Rabbi Yehuda Ashlag, in the essay "Peace in the World" claims that each of us has a certain uniqueness, and he explains this idea with a special flavor:

> Why are we special? Because the One who created us is "one, unique, and special" and no duplication emanates from Him (His production line has only "hand-made" products.)

And not only that, but we have a great responsibility, towards ourselves and towards others, to bring this special talent to fruition, and not, heaven forbid, to destroy it, and thus annul that talent or uniqueness.

Rav Kook writes:

> One must look for some special power that is embedded within them, and not throw it away... rather, they must ponder deeply, and make sure that they use it properly... thus we must understand, that anyone with some special power must actualize it as completely as possible; and if not, not only do they not derive benefit from it, but rather this power causes confusion and great loss in everything they do.

(*"Mussar Avicha" (Your Father's Ethics)*)

See what Rabbi Yehuda Ashlag writes about this:

> Thus we see that anyone who corrupts an individual's talent and uproots it from them causes the world to lose that lofty and wonderful concept which was supposed to appear at the end of the chain of generations, *because that talent will never appear again in any other body but theirs* ("Freedom").

Talent

I'll give you an example of talent.

A few years ago, on a particularly wintry and snowy day, as I warmed myself comfortably inside my down feather blanket, my cell phone rang, and on the other end was a friend. "You have to save me," he hollered, "you know that tonight I'm designing the Hanukkah event, right?" Of course I knew; I'm one of those invited. "So that's it," he continued, "I bought all the supplies I need online from a store in Jerusalem, and I have to get someone to bring me the stuff from there, otherwise the stage won't be properly decorated. Moshe, you live in Modi'in, which is the closest place to Jerusalem I know. Can you go there, get the stuff, "'skip'" it over to my wife who's at Ben-Gurion, and she'll bring me?" Well, you don't say "no" to a friend, so I threw on a light coat and drove towards the destination. At the entrance to Jerusalem, I already began to understand that I had made a mistake — it was snowing. The snow plows had pushed the snow aside, but the roads were really dangerous. When I entered the city, the situation was much worse; the snow wasn't being cleared, and the cars on the road served as the snow plows. In short, I nevertheless somehow got to the store, and when I got out of the car I made another mistake and sank my left foot into a huge puddle, but I comforted myself that the importance of the mission made the puddle worth it. I went into the store, and, with great enthusiasm, I informed the saleswoman that I was the messenger to pick up the stage decoration supplies, and I identified my friend who had bought it. "Right away," she said; then she turned around and handed me a bag. A bag? I asked myself. I came to collect stage decoration supplies; I didn't intend to risk my life for a bag. It turns out that yes, that's exactly what I did. Inside the bag were some runners, elongated fabrics that usually are used to decorate tables. I drove to Jerusalem in the snow for table runners? I shut my mouth, drove to Ben-Gurion, and handed the bag to his wife. "That's the last time I'm doing that friend a favor" I told myself.

But the story is about something else. When I entered the hall in the evening, the stage looked like a million dollars. My friend hung the runners from the ceiling downwards, almost to the floor. I remember myself seeing and not believing how talented and creative he was, and how creative and talented I wasn't, at least not at design. After all, I never dreamed that table runners could hang that way. It turned out that they didn't give him a budget, so he bought material at the cheapest store which he found online. How much money is usually invested to decorate the stage in an event of six hundred people? My friend set up the stage beautifully for $15. That's talent.

In the course of my life I've met many people who surprised me by their uniqueness: I met a guy who dreamed of developing an app for a smartphone that the user could use to scan the barcode in the supermarket, and the app would show them detailed information about the product, including lower prices available within walking distance.

I met a professor at Bar-Ilan University who has been studying cellular differentiation for decades, trying to understand how cells of the embryo divide and become different organs even though originally they were exactly alike; how in one moment, some cells become skin cells, others become teeth, even others become eyes, and so on. At this point, science can't explain how this differentiation takes place. He, this professor we know, has a talent that most of us can't comprehend: to sit in a lab and study cells.

I met someone whose talent is... finding faults. On the face of it, it would seem that this talent isn't very positive. She sees everything that is wrong with people, with her spouse, with the imperfect world we live in. What do you think? Is this a talent or not? It turns out that this woman works for the world's largest software company, and earns a beautiful salary as the manager of the company's quality control department. Not only she does a good job finding faults; I think that the State Comptroller is also pretty good at it too.

Smart people understand that there is nothing negative in reality. It all depends on how we use things.

Others Are As Talented As We Are

True, there is merit in your words, you aren't the only Shiatsu therapist in the world, so what's so special about you? Are your exercises different from those of others? And there are so many singers, service providers, salespeople, lecturers and so on.

True, but someone *exactly* like you — no. Some people will connect just to you, even if someone else does the same thing as you do, and maybe even better. And what if they have more experience than you do? It doesn't matter. Be the best you can at what you are, and there will be people who connect to your pathway and not to someone else's. This is the way of the world. Millions of people bake cookies in the world, no cookie is exactly like another, and although there will be quite a few people who will turn up their noses at your cookie – there will always be some people who will say that this is the most delicious cookie they ever tasted, as Rabbi Kook writes:

> God performed kindness with his world, in that He did not place all talents in one place, nor in one man and nor in one nation, nor in one country, nor in one generation and nor in one world, but rather, talent is dispersed, and perforce perfection is found in the transcendent unity which must come into the world.

(Orot (Lights), Orot Yisrael (Lights of Israel))

Perfection, then, will express itself when everyone will contribute from their own talents.

If I Have Several Talents – How Can I Tell Which is My Mission?

My cooking abilities are well known to hundreds of people who have tasted my wonderful creations, and yet – I'm not a cook or a chef. I invest most of my time in lectures, writing and coaching.

Why am I not a chef?

How did you decide, Mr. Moshe Sharon, that your mission is to feed the soul and not to feed the body? Why don't you open a restaurant?

How does a person know which of the areas in which they are talented is the field in which they should focus?

Here are three signs:

The First Sign – The Social Environment

In Israel, when people meet a happy person, they describe him with the Hebrew word "*meushar*," which also means "approved." This is a strange word for "happy," a word that doesn't seem at first glance to be related to the person's happiness.

What is the connection between someone's contentment and smiles and "approval"?

Who gives someone "approval" to be happy?

Well, happy is the person who radiates their qualities and talents naturally, who rejoices in them and in their surroundings - whether a singer or caretaker.

The people around them say to them, "Wow, your singing is amazing."

Or, "Since you've arrived, we send our child to kindergarten with peace of mind."

You're a bank teller. Customers insist that only you serve them; they aren't interested in talking to any other teller, even if it means they have to wait in line twice as long.

That is to say, the social environment indicates to the person, gives him "approval". Usually, approval from others makes a person happy. They are happy to have been "approved."

And vice versa – if an absolute majority of the people in your social environment indicate to you that they don't like what flows from you, and nevertheless you decide that this is your mission, then it's reasonable to assume that your ego is managing you, not your mission.

For example, if a journalist decides that his mission on this earth is to uncover all the fiascos that happened in his country, as well as the failures of the army, even if this means endangering the country's security and giving its enemies tools to destroy it, is it possible to say that his sense of mission is adequate?

If your entire environment indicates that your giving is undesirable, if your social environment doesn't "approve" of you, it looks like you aren't in the right direction (even though there are also exceptions, which have brought many innovations to a world that was too small-minded to accept them).

Is it possible that there is a person with a certain talent and that *is* their purpose, but they are in a social environment that doesn't appreciate or doesn't "approve" of it? How can we distinguish between a lack of approval which serves as a sign that this is not one's purpose or simply a non-supportive environment?

The answer is that one must distinguish between the social environment into which someone is born and the social environment within which they choose to grow. The social environment into which you were born often tries to confine you within the limits it knows, and, as a result, may not "approve" of something which threatens it. But when someone matures, they will usually choose a different social environment, one that will approve of them. In other words: Please don't break down if Father and Mother oppose...

Second Sign –By Day and By Night

I remember, for example, that on Shavuot, the Jewish holiday of the Giving of the Torah (when it's customary to learn Torah all night), I fell asleep. When I woke up, I asked myself, how was it that I fell asleep on such a meaningful night? In the middle of the celebration of the Giving of the Torah, you fall asleep? Then I realized that if I were the teacher and not the student, I wouldn't fall asleep... And indeed, the following year, the Almighty granted me the privilege of teaching Torah in the city of Hebron from 20:00 to 5:00 in the morning, non-stop. I don't know about the students, but I'm sure that at least the teacher didn't fall asleep...

If you like something, *you can do it day and night, you think about it even when you are prevented from doing it for all sorts of reasons, and wait for the time when you can finally get back to it.*

You can also look at this sign from another angle: you're the one who knows yourself. There are activities in which five minutes of doing them seem like an hour, and there are others in which an hour seems like five minutes. It's in the latter area you're probably supposed to end up. As they say, "time flies when you're having fun."

Some people like to put things together. They buy tables, sofas, armchairs, cabinets, and everything possible, but what's important to them is that they should be the kind that they have to assemble themselves at home. They can sit on the floor with screwdrivers and assembly directions for four hours, and not notice the passing time.

Once I dreamed of playing the guitar. The first lesson was interesting. I bought a guitar for the second lesson. After the third lesson, I practiced in the living room. In the fourth lesson, I complained that the pads of my fingers hurt. During the fifth lesson, I suffered and waited impatiently for it to be over. The sixth lesson never took place, to this very day. And the guitar? The guitar is in the garage.

Third Sign –Like a Flowing Spring

If this is indeed your talent, then one of the signs of this is that you will have an infinite number of creative ideas about this subject. You will be inspired, and you will have endless innovations in this field.

My wife, for example, likes knitting with tricot threads, and every time she does, a new idea comes to her for a basket or carpet. She has even knitted a bear and a turtle.

I have endless ideas for new books and courses. Sometimes I hear one lesson, or even one sentence or one quotation, and on that basis I build a new lecture or a whole course.

See how Rabbi Kook puts it:

> Whoever has the soul of a creator has to create ideas and thoughts; it is impossible for him to be confined to superficial study alone, because the flame of the soul rises spontaneously, and nothing can stop it.

(Holy Lights)

It's true that the signs I mentioned are really great signs, but nevertheless these three signs didn't help me, because in the field of cooking too I get very positive feedback from my social environment, I can cook day and night, and I have a lot of ideas... Maybe, after all, I should be a cook?

I'll answer that later, but before that, I'd better answer another question:

If we assume that we are talented in more than one field, should we focus on developing only one of them, or should we give a stage to other talents as well?

What Are You, Gentlemen? What Are You, Ladies?

What are you? Patient or impatient? Passive or active? Gentle or aggressive? Special or "like everyone else?" Brave or cowardly? Sensitive to others or egoistic?

I want to tell you a secret: *you're everything.*

If you think about it, you will see that all these qualities potentially exist in you. There are people who extract patience from you, and some who extract impatience. So what are you?

Joy and sadness are mixed up in you, so what are you? Happy or not?

You have infinite talent. It would be cruel to call you by your name or a description, such as fat, skinny, tall, short, dark-skinned or any other description. If we think about descriptions properly, we will understand that they are a kind of character assassination. When someone puts you in a mold, they don't allow you to be all that you are. You potentially have infinite abilities, skills, emotions, distinctions, innovations. You are everything, people. You aren't just hyperactive or just "ADHD." You concentrate on what interests you and don't concentrate on other things, you're sensitive in certain fields and indifferent in others. You're everything. You aren't in the humanities or in the sciences, you are in both. There are so many contradictions in you, so many aspects to you, that you really can't define one unique area or talent that you are skilled in.

Your profession isn't you either. You aren't "football players" or "Supreme Court justices." You aren't "lawyers" or "secretaries." You are *both* all these and *also* lots of other things. What is written in your horoscope is both true and false to the same degree.

But even though *you* aren't limited, *reality usually is limited.* Time is limited, mental powers are limited. Like relationships: just as when "you" are a father and "you" are a spouse and "you" a manager, you aren't the same "you," so too in every incarnation, another role is demanded of you. Your soul is constantly struggling with another part within itself.

That's why focus is important. That's why it's very important that you don't scatter your inner powers in every direction. That's why it's important to invest energies in the right place, or at the very least to stop wasting them on everything that doesn't advance you in your mission.

When water flowing in nature within a river is focused in a single channel and towards the same target, it receives tremendous power. If we split the stream into ten channels, without a doubt the river would lose some of its power.

Why Do We Waste Energies on the Negative?

Unlike what seems to us, we are all busy most of the day with what we *can't* do, with that which is difficult for us. According to studies, most people invest ninety percent of their inner energies in trying to improve on things that are difficult for them. They pity themselves, and perpetuate the problems.

"Maybe you should improve upon what you do best?" I say to the guy who is preoccupied with what *he isn't* instead of what *he is.*

"Then you will be yourself," I assert repeatedly to the trainees, "and stop being afraid of what people will say."

My girls know, for example, that if a toy breaks, or their drawer falls apart, not to ask Dad to fix it. Instead, they ask "When is Grandpa coming?" Their father doesn't mess with home repairs, he isn't the "handyman" in the house, and they don't constantly demand that he deal with what constitutes a nightmare for him. When the grandfathers come to fix things, cooking-talented Dad makes a delicious meal for them...

But wait, if I fail in something, then maybe it's part of my *tikkun*, my correction, maybe that's exactly what I need to do, to make an effort to fix the specific area in which I have difficulty? Maybe we indeed *should* make an effort to improve what we aren't good at?

The answer is in the negative. It's better to improve on what you already do well. One of the streams in positive psychology says:

Do what you do best even better.

Many people don't invest efforts in their mission because they are busy trying to improve in a field in which they aren't gifted. This is a waste of time!

The internet world in general, and the social media world in particular, are good examples: I know therapists, business owners, etc., who are very talented in their profession. However, in our current online world, those who don't know how to market themselves on social networks, those who don't bother to set up a website and maintain it, are left far behind, at the very least according to the feeling everyone gives them. So they break their backs to post a single photo in a "record time" of three hours. Believe me, even if they do study how to design a website and take courses, in most cases they will function as web designers only on a very rudimentary level, struggling with a system that speaks to them in Chinese, at least as far as it seems to them.

It's great that the Almighty, the Beneficent, made sure that there are messengers who are proficient in the field, who can do your web marketing for you with ease.

Attorney Yaniv Zaid, a persuasion doctor – that's what he calls himself – tells his listeners that an expert prepared the PowerPoint presentation he is showing them. Couldn't he have invested effort in it himself? Certainly, but the result would be mediocre. During the time an expert prepared this presentation for me, he explains, I wrote a few more chapters in my next book.

In other words, King David said: "Avoid the bad, and do

good." If you want to succeed in all areas of life, you have no choice but to focus on what you're good at, at the same time giving up on what you didn't get from above.

Rav Kook writes about our talents as follows:

Talent depends on two things:

a. Diligent study, adding knowledge and experience.

b. However, the main thing is natural talent. For if someone has natural inborn talent, their diligent study will result in greater understanding, but if someone's soul lacks natural, inborn talent, no study will ever enable him to overcome his inborn lack of ability.

And he concludes with these words:

As everyone knows, even with an enormous amount of study, a person will not become a wonderful artist or an outstanding musician, unless he was created with a natural aptitude for such things.

*(Ein Aya, **Berachot**)*

With all due respect to man's free choice, talent indicates to a person where they should position themselves, just as a lack of talent, or mediocre talent, indicates where they shouldn't position themselves.

And On The Other Hand

If I only deal with what I'm good at – isn't that a missed opportunity? Isn't this running away from commitment?

The phrase "that's how I am" for example, can drive any normal woman crazy when she hears it from her husband:

"Why don't you tell me you love me?"

"That's how I am. When you married me you knew that I don't talk about my feelings, why are you trying to change me?"

This is a relatively good answer. There are men who answer "I told you at the wedding that I love you; if there's any change, I'll let you know."

Still, if it's hard for him to speak of his feelings, why doesn't she accept him as he is?

Do I have to accept myself or to change? Isn't it a waste of energy? Let's enjoy what is, instead of spending time on what isn't.

The answer is that there is a difference between temperament and virtues - moral qualities. Your personality doesn't need to be changed, but the virtues you apply, through which your personality expresses itself, can and should be refined.

That is, if you're by nature a hot-natured, quick-thinking person who understands things quickly and reacts to things quickly – you needn't, and in any event you can't, make yourself gentle, patient and slow. On the contrary, it seems that you can perform your mission largely by virtue of that temperament.

So what should change?

If you hurt your spouses by your reactions, you should check the character trait through which you express your temperament, and be a little more patient or gentler than you have been. Anger is a good energy that is dangerous only when it appears in the incorrect character quality, as Rabbi Kook writes:

> None of all the attributes that God has created in man's nature and soul is so absolutely bad that the soul would be better off if it were utterly absent (i.e., there is no completely unnecessary trait), because God, the Good Worker, did everything for the best. We just need to

use each attribute at the proper time, and to the proper degree. From this it follows that a wicked attribute should not be pushed away too much, rejecting it entirely. *The perfect person may also be angry,* so the attribute of anger must exist, but then it is appropriate to calm down one's anger immediately. However, it's impossible to say that anger has no place at all, as if an utterly evil power was created in the soul.

(Rav Kook, *Ein Aya,* **Berachot)**

Or simply put – my recommendation is not to waste energy on what you aren't good at, but to invest your resources and energies in being the best in what you're already good at. However, my recommendation isn't an excuse for not refining your character. Refining your character is necessary in order to achieve a higher level of purity while fulfilling your purpose in life. I will deal with this at length in Chapter Five.

I Don't Fit Into Anything

They tell of a woman who used to sit in the market square. Everyone who was in trouble would come and sit by her and tell her their problems. She would contemplate their story, turning things over in her mind, and in response tell them a story. The person would roll the story around in their head, until the solution to their problem would suddenly appear before their very eyes.

One day, a woman of about forty came and sat down in front of her. "My problem is," she said, "I don't fit into anything. I tried a lot of different jobs. I lived in a lot of places. I didn't really fit in anywhere. I went out with lots of guys, but I never felt I fit in."

The storyteller answered immediately, in your case I don't even have to think, because I used to be in your condition too, but I had no one to ask, so I went out to seek the answer alone. I passed towns and villages, valleys and streams, vineyards and orchards. One day I found myself walking along the road. Fields were on the right, fields as far as the eye can see on the left, and aside from that – nothing. After walking for a few hours, I saw a wall standing at the edge of the road.

From a distance, I could see colored spots on it, some high on the wall, some low, and some scattered around in the middle. I quickly approached and stood facing the wall. Then I saw that those colored spots were targets that arrows are shot at, and in the precise center of every target, an arrow was stuck. Who could display such excellent marksmanship? I asked myself. But there was no one to ask, so I kept walking. There was a small house on the top of the hill, and in the courtyard, bent above a flowerbed, was a girl much younger than I.

I went up to her and asked her, "Do you know by chance who shot the arrows at the targets on the wall along the road?"

She got up and answered shyly, "I did."

"But how can that be?" I said skeptically. "You're so young!"

"The truth is," the young girl replied, "that first of all I shot the arrows, and then I painted the targets around them."

"I learned a lot from her answer," the storyteller told the troubled woman sitting opposite her. "I learned that first of all I had to find what was fit for me, not what I fit into. *I found what suited me, and around that, I built my life.*"

To Summarize the Third Insight

"Your Talents Hint at the Life Purpose"

- There is no completely wise person and no completely unwise person, just as there is no completely talented person and no completely untalented one. Today we know that there are different types of intelligence, and everyone is smart in a different field. The same applies to talent. No one will convince me that they aren't talented at anything.

- What right do you have to waste your talents and not implement them?

- Each of us consists of a vast array of qualities, skills, and abilities, most of which we don't know about. Any attempt to define us completely with one description is character assassination that limits and restricts us from revealing and accurately defining our mission.

- Our social environment indicates to us when it likes a trait/talent that emanates from us. It gives us its approval.

- When you "broadcast" your talents, you're in the clouds and don't notice how time passes; you're ready to give of yourself unlimitedly.

- If there is an area where you have unlimited ideas, like a flowing spring, you should be aware that your mission is probably there.

- Even though you're talented in certain areas and a failure in others – you can't afford to waste precious time repairing everything you aren't good at; this is futile. Doing the opposite is correct – you should take the subject that you're good in and upgrade it to the limit, and not waste energy on other topics. Do what you do best even better.

- Everyone has one talent or several talents, but it turns out that talent alone can't provide final confirmation of the question, what is the exact mission for whose sake you reached the world? For that we need a fourth insight: failure.
- If you aren't familiar with it yet – search YouTube for the song "Kanfei ruach" composed Binny Landau to the words written by Rabbi Kook: Ascend, ascend, for you have fierce power. You have wings of wind, wings of noble eagles. Do not deny them, lest they deny you. Look for them, and you will find them immediately.

Exercise for the Thirds Insight– Talents

1. The people around me indicate that they like it when I
    _____ and _____

2. In the area _____
    _____ I have a lot of ideas.

3. I can spend long hours doing _____ and ___
    _____ without noticing.

4. Think about three success stories from the past or the
    present that you're happy about/proud of. The success
    story doesn't have to be huge, even "small" successes in the
    interpersonal sphere are successes; the condition is that
    you're proud of them. Now, think about five attributes/
    abilities *of yours* that made each success possible: Good
    human relations? Broad vision? Perfectionism? Please
    name five attributes for each story, for a total of fifteen
    attributes and abilities:

Story #1	Story #2	Story #3

From what you understand, what do you estimate is your talent or talents? _____

_____

This Insight Wouldn't be Complete Without the Following Story:

They tell of a twenty-six-year-old with an outstanding management, academic and business record who received an offer to manage one of the largest advertising agencies in Israel – although he totally lacked any background in advertising.

As a serious guy, he took the job.

He decided that during the first week he would interview all the workers and get to know them up close. He sat down and formulated a structured interview with many questions. On the morning of the first day, the first employee came in:

"What complex projects are you working on?" was the opening question.

The interviewee in front of him responded to the interviewer's question with great seriousness, but with reluctance.

The next question was: "What are the greatest difficulties in your job?"

Again, the interviewer replied politely but with an obvious lack of enthusiasm.

Then the transformation took place.

Somehow they began to talk about the things the interviewee liked to do with their life.

"Suddenly the man changed right in front of me. His bearing became lively, his face filled with a smile, his eyes shone, his voice became clear and alive... As an interviewer, I didn't understand exactly what was happening, and that's how the conversation flowed until the end of the interview," the manager of the advertising agency related.

According to him, the interviewee came out with high spirits, but our interviewer felt sorry and disappointed how, with all the questions he prepared, he managed to ask only two of them, and ruined the entire interview...

Before he could breathe, the next interviewee came in and the story repeated itself: the conversation spilled over into what excited the interviewee, who became full of vitality when he spelled out what things turn him on...

At the end of the two interviews, our manager had a bad feeling, and to calm down, he went out to eat something. Then, like in the cartoons, a light bulb went on over his head. Suddenly he realized if these are the questions that turn people on, it's really worthwhile to start with them.

The next interview began with the question: "I'm very curious to hear what you're enthusiastic about in life?" and he went on to ask "And if your life was a plan that went just as you wished, what would it look like?" And at the end of the interview, he delivered the punch line: "And what, of all these things, can you apply to this firm – here in your place of work?"

FOURTH INSIGHT

EVEN FAILURE CONNECTS TO YOUR MISSION

In the end, it will be known,
There is no evil.
Only seemingly.

(Rabbi Moshe Chaim Luzzatto — the Ramchal, *Adir*
*Bamarom II, Reisha and Seifa***)**

Just as every person has received one or more talents with which they can influence others, so too, if we look carefully, there seems to be no one who has experienced no failure, who can say that there isn't at least one thing that they failed at again and again.

It seems that, as with talents, our failures are also unique: some people destroy their lives with cigarettes, some buy luxuries and run up debts and foreclosures. There are those who can't see good in anything, some people have no self-confidence; there are those who don't succeed in relationships — for them, relationships are one big failure. Throughout their lives, they suffer; they make an effort, yet fail to find their chosen partner. What seems simple to other people is complex and traumatic for them.

Moreover, most of the time, it's hard for us to understand our friends' failures, for example, speaking in front of an audience. In a famous study, hundreds of thousands of participants were asked: What is your biggest fear? The most common answer was speaking in front of an audience. The second most common answer was death. The comedian Jerry Seinfeld stated that, if so, most people would rather be the one in the coffin than the one delivering the eulogy...

I ask myself: Why are people so afraid of speaking to an audience? It's fun, challenging, stimulating, empowering, no?

People may answer: You're a wise guy, Moshe Sharon, with your special mix of abilities that you received from Above; the ability to speak in front of an audience belongs to the category of talent, but not everyone is like you...

Since the word "failure" has different aspects, we should put things in perspective.

Failure can appear in four different ways:

a. **A desire you can't overcome,** such as, for example, for food, or for money. As the Admor of Slonim writes:

> It is written in the holy books that each person has a mission for which he has descended into the world, a special matter that God has given him which must correct, and this his mission on earth. The way to know what a person's special mission, the sign of it, is that, in regard to this, *the evil inclination most intensely tempts him.*

(Netivot Shalom)

b. **A personality trait that you can't fix**, such as anger, control, pride, envy, self-confidence, and others.

c. **An area that you find very difficult**, such as difficulty in finding or maintaining relationships.

d. **A traumatic event from the past that shaped you**, such as a crisis, the death of parents at an early age, injury, and others. Here, of course, this isn't something which you yourself personally failed at, but it's also included under the heading "failure."

An Example of Section A — desire — Moshe Sharon's Failure

If we take my failure as an example, then I have one major one: food. I'm someone who succeeds in almost everything he touches, thank God. To me, sometimes this failure, food, seems illogical, because I consider myself a sensible person with common sense; I understand one or two things in life, and I've helped other people lose weight. However, when it comes to me, I succeed and fail intermittently. Mostly I fail. Even if I succeed in eating healthy food, for example, then the amount is excessive.

Lord of the Universe, what do you want from me? Some people don't obsess over food, and some sometimes even forget to eat. Why do I keep thinking about food? Why am I stuck with those extra pounds? Instead of exercising five times a week and investing hours preparing healthy food for myself, I could use my time to write books to help others. Why have you have put me in this prison?

Indeed, I asked this question, and have even received quite a few answers.

But believe it or not, failure brings with it several gifts

necessary for the mission. Ever since I found the answer to this question, I give thanks every day for my failure. Further on I will describe in detail the gifts that failure brings.

Example of Section B – personality trait — Tammy

Tammy is fifty-two years old and her greatest desire is to put into practice the knowledge she acquired.

And what did you study? I asked.

I studied parental guidance at the Adler Institute.

For three years I studied the Elbaum Method, which deals with helping children with motor problems.

I learned NLP.

I learned "By way of the artist" — a writing therapy method.

I learned coaching.

I studied group facilitation and...

Wow, I said, really excited, it's great for you, and for the world, that you have all this knowledge and all these skills.

Yes, but I don't work at counseling; I work as a cashier at a supermarket.

A cashier at a supermarket? Why?

I'm really helpless, I'm unable to tell people I'm a therapist, and to advertise or promote myself. I'm a disaster at social media.

"The eternal students" I often call those who continue to train themselves without any purpose. I said to Tammy, I don't understand, so what did you do with all your diplomas? Put them in a drawer?

I don't have any diplomas. Not one. I get stressed out before exams, and I don't take them.

***

I think you get the idea. There are people with excessive self-confidence, who take one lesson in Chinese medicine and immediately begin to stab the whole family with Chinese needles as if they were masters. On the other hand, there is Tammy, who has so much to offer, but is afraid of her own shadow.

In both cases, the failure is in "how much." Self-confidence isn't a completely bad thing, just as a lack of self-confidence isn't completely bad either; both of these have a certain charm, both of these are necessary. This kind of failure must serve the person's mission.

Example of Section C – area – Leah's Children and Naama's Children

Leah was a young ultra-Orthodox woman who married at the age of nineteen. She grew up in a family of thirteen in which she didn't lack anything, materially or spiritually. Full of joy, she began planning her own family, but God's intention was apparently different from hers; for several years, Leah coped with an expectation for children that was unfulfilled.

Those who are even a little familiar with the Haredi, ultra-Orthodox world know that the social aspect of childlessness multiplies the difficulty. Within a short time, Leah went from a successful woman to a pitiful "delayed" one, for whom everyone should pray every day, prostrate themselves on the graves of the righteous, in accordance with Jewish custom, and light candles. Fear of her husband's reaction echoed in the background; would he abandon her because of her infertility?

Eight years later, when she embraced her eldest daughter, she publicly declared that she was thankful for those eight years. Why? Because, according to her, those years sent her a lesson in gratitude. I didn't appreciate anything in life, she said, because everything I wanted came to me easily; now I appreciate things. Was the failure in the area of fertility necessary in Leah's case?

Na'ama isn't married, and very much wants children. "But because of my age," she said with a bitter smile, "I won't have any. At least not any of my own."

I wanted to encourage her, but then she encouraged me. She said she was a volunteer at a local hospital to hug children and abandoned babies. She hugs nearly forty children every visit.

Did you know there was a possibility to embrace children as a volunteer? Could it be that the Higher Power, who is responsible for the overall picture, has made it so that there are women whose job it is to be the mother of three or four children, and other women whose job it is to be the "mother" of forty children?

In both these examples, failure is in a certain area of life. Even though someone succeeds in everything else, in this area they experience endless failure.

Example of Section D — The trauma of Dmitry/ David

A classic example of a traumatic life-shaping event: Thirty-five, years ago, Dmitri worked in a factory in Russia. He definitely won't forget the "significant" event that shaped his life. He was only twenty, working at a cutting machine in a factory, and debating in his mind whether or not to accept an offer to join an LSD party that he was invited to in the evening. As he was thinking about this, the palm of his hand got caught in the machine and cut off. That evening, instead of taking drugs in a forest, he found himself in the hospital, in excruciating pain, with a Jewish nurse taking care of him.

He fell in love with the nurse in a way he never thought

possible, and was prepared to convert to marry her. Fast forward. Today, Dmitri lives in Jerusalem with his wife; on their door are written names that almost completely cover up any trace of what happened in Russia. David and Talia are an ultra-Orthodox couple, parents of seven children, and feel on the top of the world. When David tells the story, he gets excited and his eyes light up. "Just imagine, if my hand hadn't been cut off, where would I be today? Taking drugs?"

In this case, the failure isn't a personal failure, but rather a traumatic event. We'll encounter a traumatic event in the story about the messenger "who doesn't have any talent at all" further on in this book.

So there are different types of failure. How is my failure connected to my mission?

Your failure contains within it innumerable gifts, for your lives in general, and your mission in particular:

Gift # 1: Thanks to Failure, You Need Others

It's amazing: when you fail in a particular area, you need someone else. Or more precisely, you need the talent, the mission of the other person. My failure enlivens, enables, and makes room for other people's giving.

Just as my talent is designed to give others what they need, so my failure is intended, among other things, to allow other messengers to give me what I need from them.

Yuval's Failure

Yuval was wounded in the army. He was hospitalized and confined to rehabilitation centers for a long time. During that time, he discovered that he wanted to heal himself. He flew to the United States and studied medicine. Through Yizhar, the occupational therapist who treated him after the injury, he discovered Chinese and natural medicine, bonded with its messages, and trained himself for years in Chinese medicine and nutrition, in a method called "natural hygiene." Yuval's failure transformed him into someone with a need for Yizhar's talent.

King David said, Go and make a living from each other (2 Samuel 8). And indeed, if you think about it, people help one another in areas in which each of them is weak. Everyone has different kinds of needs: mental, physiological, emotional. Because of these needs, people help one another, the economy thrives, and thus most people are able to make a living. This is amazing.

But that's not the end of the story:

Since returning to Israel, besides treating thousands of people, Yuval saved hundreds of patients from cancer and diabetes through natural nutrition, without using even one drug. Yuval also established a school for alternative medicine, and trains therapists.

Yuval's mission is apparently to heal people, and more importantly, to teach them how to heal themselves with grapes, carrots, lettuce, and broccoli.

He Who summoned Yuval's injury and recovery, He Who instilled skills and knowledge in him, wanted Yuval to bring relief to those who needed him, wanted Yuval to be a fitting conduit for those in need, and even, in certain cases, to those who had given up on Western medicine which gave no relief to the blow that had fallen upon them.

A point to consider: Is it possible to say that Yuval couldn't have reached his destiny without having been injured in the army? When that happened, he and his family must have been shocked by that "fate" that struck them, but if you look at things in perspective, can't you say that the injury was necessary for Yuval's mission?

Gift # 2: Failure Produces Humility

Here's another benefit: Not only do I, Moshe Sharon, need Yuval to help me with eating, at the same time I also put things in perspective: I'm not perfect! Thanks to failure and my need for others, I correct the trait of conceit that may arise in me in my role as an inspiration and a messenger, whom others can't do without.

Be aware: you can't exist without other people.

In my training room, I meet psychologists, dentists, business people, rabbis and countless successful "persona." In internal contemplation, each and every one of them admits their limitations, their "low" moments. Each and every one of them, just before they go to sleep, knows how imperfect they are, and how much work awaits them. How amazing.

The one who once expressed this "picturesquely" was no other than the basketball player Michael Jordan:

> *"I missed more than 9,000 shots in my career. I lost almost 300 games. 26 times I had to throw the winning shot and missed. I have failed again and again in my life. And that's why I succeeded."*

Gift # 3: Thanks to Failure, You Can Relate To/ Understand the Failure of Others, and Help Them

When I sit in front of a guy who doesn't have a partner, who is having trouble developing a relationship, who doesn't succeed in complimenting the girl he is interested in — how can I really understand him? How can I understand his difficulty, if I never experienced it myself, if I never felt as he did? The fact that I have failures lets me relate to his.

My wife, for example, has a hard time coping with driving outside the city. She literally shakes with fear.

"What's the problem with driving outside of the city?" I ask myself. I was never afraid of driving; how can I understand her?

The answer is that just as you have a hard time with chocolate, she has a hard time with highway driving.

Instead of patronizing her and treating her like a coward, my failure allows me to understand her and maybe even help her. I myself have experienced that it's not helpful to be told that "you have to," or that it's not healthy, or that I overdo things.

Imagine that we would never have experienced failure; how would we understand someone else's crisis/difficulty? How would we help them? We would look at them with pity and not understand what is so difficult for them.

Someone who provides service, for example, should ask themselves, what is most important to the person being served? Is it important for them to be listened to, to the end? Is it that the server shows willingness to move heaven and earth for them? That they don't give them the feeling that they are "just a number"? That they smile at them? That they don't let them wait too long? Whatever the answer is, that's exactly the service that the service provider must give.

Gift #4: Your Failure and That of Others are Interrelated

Look at something amazing: I train people "one-on-one," or, as we used to say, "face-to-face." Sometimes someone sits down in front of me, and I don't understand why they came. How can I help them?

I turn to God and say to Him: "Listen, God, the fact that I have learned to coach, doesn't mean that I can help all the people in the world. Show me the way."

At that moment, two things emerge:

1. I discover how it's possible to help that person.

2. I find that it wasn't just the Almighty who sent them to me. What they tell me, even if it's a completely different story than mine, mirrors an area that I need to work on myself. They pay me money, but really I should pay them. Couples sit opposite me, and it's unbelievable that God sent me people with the exact issue that, at this minute, is unfolding between me and my wife. The conclusion is that the inner world radiates outwards, and presents me with exactly what I need to be aware of, and to correct.

Gift # 5: Failure reminds you of the Higher Source

An old joke tells of a guy who is looking for parking for an hour and can't find one. At one point, he raises his eyes to heaven and says, "God, help me, I give up, I can't find any parking. If You send me a parking spot, I'll start observing Shabbat." And then, he looks down and suddenly sees the vehicle in front of him pulling out and leaving a parking spot. He immediately looks heavenward again and says, "Thanks, God, no need for Your help, I managed by myself."

The truth is that the joke is about us. When the things in our lives are going okay — who needs Him? Only when someone is close to surgery does everybody start praying.

Failure connects us to the Higher Power, to God. Why? Because when you fail, you realize that you aren't all-powerful. I may think I'm some kind of important guy, but then a piece of chocolate comes and shows me who I really am...

Pharaoh, the most arrogant person of all time, thought he was a god, and that's what he told the Egyptian people — The River Nile is mine, and I created myself. The Sages say that he would refrain every day from relieving himself, so that his people won't wonder how this "god" behaves just like us, like human beings, and so he would sneak to the Nile at daybreak, when everyone slept, to relieve himself in secret.

The Creator *has* to send us failure, so that conceit doesn't overwhelm us. Thus, failure is necessary to connect a person with God, so that the person will need not only others, but God as well.

Without failure, we would become Pharaoh, arrogant and stubborn. We would be sure that we are gods.

Repeated failures, diseases or traumatic events are supposed, according to Rav Kook, to inspire you. Disease, for example, is intended to soften our "stiff-necks."

Disease acts positively on the human character; through it, man surrenders to God, and mankind's knowledge of the possibility of illness works for the good, to soften the stubbornness of stiff-necked people, and to rectify the hearts of malicious ones. Indeed, to complete the positive lesson that a person receives from the reality of illness, man needs by his nature to pray, to beseech the Lord to save him in times of trouble.

(Ein Aya)

So, yes, failure is intended to make us remember, and turn to, the Higher Power. It reminds us that we aren't alone here; it's a positive reminder. But most people don't understand the "language" the reminder is written in, so they run towards every possible solution (except to contact the Higher Power), just so as not to feel the pain: anti-depressants, drugs, cigarettes, alcohol, shopping, carbs, television – none of which transforms failure into success, quiets the inner cry nor the desires, and so, the failure has been made even deeper and more difficult to overcome.

If I put the Higher PowerHigher Power into the picture, then every time I receive a blow, I immediately understand that the blow came from Him. True, it's possible that at the moment someone specific hit me, insulted me, but ultimately, even the person who struck me is only a messenger.

I have two options: either to fight the messenger or to understand that it's a reminder to re-connect with the Higher Power. If I choose the first option I get annoyed, act dramatically, and am confident that this is all there is to reality. According to the second option, I know that I don't know everything now, but I do know that someday I'll understand. I'll probably find out then that I had to undergo this lesson, this "evil," in order to advance toward the mission which was already known to the Higher Power, but was hidden from me.

Remember Dmitry's story?

We can delve into a wonderful example written by Rabbi Ashlag:

A parable: A king was very pleased with one of his servants, whom he wanted to promote and make senior to all the other ministers, because he recognized that this servant had an undying love for the king. But it violated the rules of the kingdom to elevate someone all at once, for no apparent reason. Rather, the kingdom's protocol required that everyone should be able to see the deep wisdom behind such a move.

What did he do? He entrusted the servant with the task of being the gatekeeper (to guard the king). Then the king told a minister, one with great acting ability, to disguise himself as a rebel against the king, and to attack the palace at a time when there were no armed guards ready to defend against such an attack.

The minister did as the king commanded, and with great skill and tactics pretended to attack the palace. The servant who was guarding the palace acted with great bravery, allowed the king to escape, and fought against the attacking minister with great heroism and tremendous devotion, until all his heartfelt love was revealed to everyone.

Then the minister took off his disguise and the matter became a big joke (because the servant fought valiantly and bravely, and now he realized that the whole thing was just an act). And everyone laughed even more when the minister described in detail the depths of the deception, the cruelty of the attacker that the servant imagined, and the imaginary fear the servant felt. The servant felt that the point of every detail of this terrible battle was to play a joke him, to everyone's entertainment. After all, he is just a servant, and how could he be made superior to all the ministers and servants of the king?

The king thought, and then told the minister that he now must disguise himself as a robber and a murderer, and attack the guard. For the king knew that in the second battle, the guard will display amazing wisdom which will make him deserve leading all the other ministers.

Therefore, the king appointed the servant to be responsible for the royal treasure (promoted him). Then the minister disguised himself this time as a cruel murderer who came to raid the King's treasures. The poor appointed servant fought with him with all his might and devotion, until things were desperate. Then the minister took off his disguise, and there was even more laughter than before, for the minister's deceptions, in all their details, provoked much amusement, since this time he had to be even cleverer than previously, for it was obvious that there was no vicious attacker in the country, and all the supposed attackers are nothing but actors.

(Rabbi Yehuda Ashlag, Pri Hacham - Iggrot)

Just a moment, while someone is fighting the battles of life, dealing with domestic and external enemies, the Higher Power laughs? To someone viewing this from the side, this seems sadistic, cruel, abusive for its own sake.

Why does a mother who is teaching her son to walk, step back every time he takes one step toward her? To the observer, she may look really cruel, *but we know she loves him.* Because of her love, she takes a step backward. She allows him to err, fall, and cope.

Then, yes, the more blows that a person experiences in their life, *the more internal or external crises they have to deal with — the greater their mission is.* When you want to train a soldier to function in a rear unit, a month's training may be enough, but when you come to train a combat soldier to be capable of penetrating the enemy command station at the critical time of battle — even a year of training isn't enough.

And what exactly happens during this military "training"? In one word: abuse. In every possible way, the soldier's superiors mistreat him; they throw him in the middle of nowhere and require him to navigate through it with minimal means. They make him undergo a grueling journey with weight on his back which makes no sense, etc.

If so, why, when the army Chief of Staff decides to "abuse" his soldiers, to turn Innocent eighteen-year-olds with "milk on their lips" into combat machines, we then give him awards for excellence, and why, when the main Higher Power, who is located far above the army Chief of Staff, decides to help us grow up and mature, do we whine?

The next parable, from the Maharal, seems to explain more than anything the added value of failure:

A parable of a flesh and blood king who gave someone a bowl to keep, and the bowl cracked. He was very upset about this, for he feared what the king would do if he found out that he had cracked the bowl. He didn't know what to do, so he decided to ask a wise man. The sage answered that a bowl in this condition is not appropriate for a king, and thus can't be returned to the king in its present condition. And he still didn't know what to do, but he thought that perhaps the wise man does not know the king's practice, so he decided to ask one of the king's confidants. The confidant replied "I know the greatness and the stature of the king — it is not proper to bring this bowl to him; it should be completely done away with (It would be better for you to throw the cracked bowl away than to return it in this condition to the king). Now he still did not know what to do, and so he said: I will go to a craftsman; he might find a way to fix it. He went to the craftsman, who said that the bowl could be fixed, but the repair would be difficult, and only part of the crack could be fixed, not all of it.

And then he said to himself, "in any event, I won't be able to completely fix the bowl; I will go to the king himself, and he will do what he wants." (So he went to the king with the cracked bowl, and amazingly) the king said, "This bowl? I can use it as it is, even cracked." (You thought that I need it in perfect condition?) And the others who didn't tell you this, did so out of respect for me, and not really according to my needs; I can use the bowl as it is.

(Netivot Olam, Netiv HaTshuva A.)

The moral is, we imagine that the King's palace is perfect, with everything in pristine condition, but the truth is that the palace is full of cracked bowls like us, who undergo failure, traumas, and blows. Why?

Because only in this way can He use us, otherwise we would be conceited and convinced that we ourselves are gods. Next time you feel bad because of your failures, remember the King:

This bowl? I can use it even cracked.

Everything is Precise

If everything that you and I experience is necessary for the mission, and if all the defects and problems in reality exist so that the emissaries can carry out their mission, then surely all that happens is supposed to happen, and it's even incredibly precise.

Rabbi Ashlag comes to the obvious conclusion:

Hence the key to understanding the weakness of those that arose in previous generations who would repair the world is that they saw man as a machine that doesn't work properly and needs repair. That is, it is necessary to remove the broken parts and replace them with others. Those who would repair the world think that problems, failures, and defects are negative, things to remove, the same way doctors surgically remove the tonsils or the appendix (before the development of inflammation) thinking that they aren't needed. For the whole purpose of those who would repair the world is to eradicate all evil and all harm in man. And the truth is that if the Creator had not impeded their actions, they would have been able by a long time ago to sift people as if with a sieve, leaving only the good and useful.

Isn't it positive to have only the good and useful?

This is exactly what they tried to do in Nazi Germany: to kill the mentally and physically challenged, to develop a human species that has no defects. They received these ideas from "enlightened" philosophy, and from the Greek Spartans' way of thinking.

Continuation of the quotation:

But the Creator maintains all the details of His creation with extreme care, and does not allow anyone to destroy anything in his possession, *but rather only to perfect and refine it*, therefore: all the world repairers of the said species will vanish from the world — the "beautiful souls" who try to disturb the Creator will disappear, but the evil traits in the world will not disappear from the world. They exist, and they count the number of steps of the necessary development that they still must overcome — until they reach their final stage.

In the previous chapter, we concluded that character traits should be refined, to the right measure. Rabbi Ashlag adds another distinction: Even if the traits look especially bad, it's just a matter of time. You must not destroy them. They also have a role. You can tone them to an effective measure.

Then, those evil traits reverse themselves, and become beneficial virtues, as the Creator intended from the start. This is similar to the fruit which sits on the branches of the tree, waiting and counting the needed days and months, until it matures, when its taste and sweetness will be revealed to every person.

(Peace in the world)

I once heard that in the perfume industry, the active, aromatic substance is the horrible scent of the skunk. For what purpose? So that the fragrance of the perfume remains on the skin longer. Even a foul smell can have a positive effect.

And what are we missing? Patience with the process the banana undergoes, and I do too — until I completely mature.

From my experience of working with people, I can testify that finding the mission is reinforced and emotionally validated, precisely when it's connected to failure.

A mission isn't one-valued or one-dimensional, so it isn't revealed *only* by way of talent or *only* by way of failure. My mission contains a "basket" of experiences, which is usually composed of several different colors of yarn: characteristics, achievements, talents, significant events, failures, fears, "pits" that I repeatedly fall into — all together these make up my puzzle. Only the sum of all these components will give us a clear picture of the mission.

So far we have dealt with defining the concept of failure and the accompanying gifts, but can failure itself become my mission? The answer is, not always, but sometimes, indeed yes. Sometimes the failure itself is the mission. For example, in the following cases:

Odelia's Failure

I once sat facing Odelia, a woman in her fifties, who told me the following story: Odelia has been a widow for many years; her husband died of cancer. Her children grew up, and one day she met a very wealthy widower, who became her partner, and told her, a few months after they met, that his late wife had died of cancer, and that he wants to establish an organization that will support the families of cancer victims and relieve their mental suffering. "I'll put this plan into practice only if you tell me that you agree to run the organization," he told Odelia.

On the one hand, she debated in her mind, together with me, this is definitely something wonderful, and I understand that this organization, this role, would make an infinitely greater contribution to society and to others than my present work as a real estate agent.

On the other hand, I had no idea how frightening it is to deal with cancer patients, or their families. Since my husband passed away more than fifteen years ago, I never went near support groups. I wanted to disengage, to move away, to forget what happened, instead of sinking into the past.

The question arises: was her meeting the rich widower accidental? Was it just by chance that they were both widowed spouses of people who died from the terrible disease?

You'll surely say, "but wait a minute, you said that if something is Odelia's mission then she would love the thing and want to do it more and more, whereas in this case, it's clear that she doesn't!"

Then Odelia and I gauged her inner emotions, all her inner voices and some repressed history. She told me that when her husband died, she felt she had come back to life quickly after the loss; she chose to live and raise two children with joy and goodness, to move forward vigorously, and not to fall into the obsession with death.

As she spoke, she suddenly realized that it was just this, the choice of life, that she wants to give to these people who didn't die physically, but kill themselves emotionally after their loved ones pass away.

To my great satisfaction, they established the organization, and it's helping families to this day.

Is it possible that our mission is located precisely in the place we are most likely to flee from?

Odelia has the skills and qualities needed to succeed in her task, together with fears and "screens" that impeded her vision. Our joint clarification process helped her see the main point: I have a mission here, I was elected, even if I didn't choose to be.

Moshe Rabbeinu's (Moses') "Failure"

At the beginning of the book of Exodus, we encounter Moshe Rabbeinu, the future leader of the people of Israel, at the beginning of his life, in a basket, too young to understand that he had been saved from the destruction that Pharaoh decreed against the Jewish male children, the very same Pharaoh in whose house he subsequently grew up.

When he grew up, he found himself, after fleeing Egypt and Pharaoh, standing in front of a burning bush which wasn't consumed. He received an enormous task: to confront Pharaoh, and to lead the Jewish people. His response was clear-cut: I'm not suitable for the task. Who am I? Maybe it's better to send someone else? Maybe Aaron, my brother?

> Who am I to go to Pharaoh, and to take the people of Israel out of Egypt?

> *(Exodus 3)*

Rabbi Shimshon Raphael Hirsch explains Moshe's answer:

> You gave me an enormous, double task, to meet two challenges: to completely overcome Pharaoh, and to lead Israel. I find within myself no strength, no shadow of talent for such a task (He has a lot of talent — but is he a leader?)

Indeed, Rabbi Samson Raphael Hirsch agrees with him:

> Anyone who has such a task placed before him is entitled to ponder it deeply. If it only concerned him, Moshe would have made every conceivable effort,

If, for example, God would instruct him to sacrifice Gershom, his son, in a way similar to Abraham's sacrifice of Isaac, he would be willing to do so, but the future of the entire nation depended on the success of his mission, for better or for worse.

Indeed, Moses was right, since the situation of the people of Israel worsened after he went to Pharaoh.

> Moses, who was "the humblest of men on the earth" (Numbers 12: 3) knew very well that he had nothing of the charismatic personality of those who inspire the masses, leaders of armies and nations, heroes and rulers. (He was speech-challenged), and this was just one reason why he couldn't lead. He was less trained for this mission than anyone else.

> It was legitimate that such a man be deterred, while amazed at the unexpected task, even if the mission was placed on him by God Wasn't it possible that the entire operation would fail because of his inadequacy, his ambivalence, his indecision vis-a-vis Pharaoh, and wouldn't then his own people suffer a terrible setback?

In a generation where leaders are chosen according to their charisma, and not according to their traits of mercy or humility, it makes no sense to send an inappropriate person on this mission.

God answered him:

> "This is the sign that I have sent you, (that is, this defect, that you see in yourself, *is what makes you fit for the task:*) for you are well aware that you have no spark of talent which will enable you to carry out, and certainly not to successfully complete, this task with your own, human ability; and since that deficiency is so obviously ingrained in your character, precisely because of this no one is more worthy than you of being the subject of my mission. I need a man who is the wisest of all men, yet at the same time the humblest of all men.

This significant flaw in you, that is, the absence of sweeping charisma that characterizes leaders, your "charismatic failure," will impact on this operation, which I will execute through you, the Exodus from Egypt and the establishment of Israel as a people, will be a "sign" for generations to come, "that I sent you" that all you will do was done as My agent, through My power.

(Rabbi Samson Raphael Hirsch, Exodus 3)

What is better? That Pharaoh should think that you're taking the Jewish people out of Egypt by virtue of your leadership charisma? That the people of Israel think that *you* took them out? The Sages so internalized this message that they decided not to put Moshe's name in the Passover Haggadah. *Your inadequacy is a divine letter of credentials*

The story of Moshe Rabbeinu wonderfully exemplifies how someone's mistaken perceptions about their mission, their imaginary fears, their "failure" — in this case, a lack of charisma — actually *served* them on the mission, rather than detracting from it.

Hodaya's Failure

Hodaya is an extraordinarily special woman. She's very sensitive, very creative, and has been bulimic since the age of sixteen. Today she is thirty-five, and in our first conversation she told of quite a few insights she learned from life, from bulimia, and from hospitalizations. The first thought in my mind, as I sat across from her, was, "Poor thing, how much she had to go through at such a young age." The second thought was: "Wow, her insights can help mothers and girls, entire families who are coping with bulimia. She never forgot one anecdote or tool that either helped her or upset her."

Could it be that Hodaya had to go through all this suffering in order to be able to help other bulimics? Is it possible to say that Linor Abergil, a beauty queen, had to go through rape in order to then go from one school to another in Israel and tell her story to young girls, to give them the strength to complain and not blame themselves? This is a shocking thought.

I remember that the first time I met her, Odelia made a painful statement which is hard to forget. "If I don't force myself to vomit, I'll be fat." Do people get fat because they don't vomit, or because they stop at a bakery and buy forty pastries and eat them in one night? To us the answer is obvious, but her head thinks differently than ours does. Hodaya claimed to me that even today she has moments that she forces herself to vomit; it's not like before, but still, how could she help others before she herself was completely cured?

Nevertheless, Hodaya learned to be a teacher and a coach, and today she helps bulimic girls. Even though she hasn't yet fully healed, and though she isn't a psychologist with forty years of experience, nevertheless, she's very successful, because she knows something that no one else knows: she knows what makes you push a finger down your throat and make yourself throw up.

Summary of the Fourth Insight:

"Failure Also Hints at the Mission":

- It's impossible that failure isn't related to mission. Failure can't be simply coincidental, accidental. You didn't experience the trauma you experienced in your childhood for no reason; a person's father didn't get cancer for no reason. In general, there is no such thing as "for no reason." Every psychologist, and certainly every man of spirit, understands this.

- The perception of failure as part of the mission helps people to see the broader picture, how everything you went through was necessary. The immediate result of such a view on your life is joy, gratefulness, understanding, acceptance and even the justification of Divine judgment. As the *Mishna* says in Tractate *Berachot* (9:5): A person must bless the Lord for the evil which befalls him just as he blesses Him for the good.

- We understand that all the experiences the Director planned for us were remarkably accurate — directed precisely at the mission for which we have gone down into the world.

- There is no point and need to eradicate "evil," but rather only to use it for the mission.

- When a person finds their destiny, they discover how everything that they have undergone through their life, all the negative or positive events, everything that happened to them, were sewn together for their mission, for the *tikkun*, the correction, the repair, for which they came down into the world. Everything they experienced, met, and felt, was necessary for the mission; otherwise, why did the Higher Power make them undergo this crisis, what's the point? The Higher Power isn't a sadist; the suffering wasn't in vain.

See how Rabbi Kook puts it:

> Because we must not attribute to "coincidence" anything from which we can derive a moral profit that perfects our shortcomings. How could any wise person consider saying that there is something from we can draw moral perfection, that was not purposely created with the highest wisdom to benefit us in our lives, as we perfect our true humanity?

How can one even think that reality is chaotic? If the human body, for example, would act without a guiding hand, without an operating intelligence, without tremendous wisdom that manages it, chaotic reality might make sense. But our eyes see the genius of the body's systems, the complexity of every detail in nature, the exact and critical distance the earth is from the sun, not too close and not too far away, so that life can exist here. Is it all coincidental?

And my life? Coincidental? And yours? For example, how can you think that your parents moved from house to house, together with you, twelve times "accidentally?" That the fact that you've lived in different countries, that you've absorbed different cultures, but that you didn't have friends all in one place, is accidental? How can you think this is just because your father was an ambassador? That isn't the real reason, but only its expression. The world has sewn together for you, and for you, and you too, for all of you and for each one a unique reality.

- The following isn't true of everyone, but you have noticed that in my case, failure and talent are in the same place? What do you mean the same place? you ask. The answer is, in the mouth. As the proverb goes, both life and death depend on the tongue.

Still, the question remains: if my failure is related to food, and my talent for cooking is no less than my talent for teaching, then why should I be a teacher and a writer rather than a chef?

The answer lies in the exercise of the first chapter, when we dealt with the question "What bothers you most? What would you fix?"

Why am I not a chef?

Because correcting a lack of good food isn't as meaningful to me, and doesn't motivate me as much, as helping couples in crisis.

The thought that I've been given the ability to help marital harmony, even a little, makes me wake up in the morning with the feeling that I am meaningful and needed in the world.

Exercise for the Fourth Insight — Failure/Crisis/Difficulty

Is there any subject in your life that you struggled with over and over again? That you fail at over and over again? Have you ever experienced a great failure in your life? Something that you wanted and couldn't achieve?

What is it? _____

What did you learn from the failure?

a. _____

b. _____

c. _____

What did the failure save you from?

_____

Was the failure something necessary for your personality?

_____

Can you find a possible connection between the failure and your mission?

_____

_____

_____

_____

Did the failure make you look/connect to the Higher Power? If so — how?

_____

The Fourth Insight isn't Complete Without the Following Speech:

In June 2005, about a year after he was diagnosed with the cancer that would ultimately kill him six and a half years later, Steve Jobs, one of the founders of Apple, gave a lecture to the students at Stanford University:

I am honored to be with you today at your commencement from one of the finest universities in the world. I never graduated from college. Truth be told, this is the closest I've ever gotten to a college graduation. Today I want to tell you three stories from my life. That's it. No big deal. Just three stories.

The first story is about connecting the dots.

I dropped out of Reed College [Portland, Oregon] after the first six months, but then stayed around as a drop-in for another 18 months or so before I really quit. So why did I drop out?

It started before I was born. My biological mother was a young, unwed college graduate student, and she decided to put me up for adoption. She felt very strongly that I should be adopted by college graduates, so everything was all set for me to be adopted at birth by a lawyer and his wife. Except that when I popped out they decided at the last minute that they really wanted a girl. So my parents, who were on a waiting list, got a call in the middle of the night asking: "We have an unexpected baby boy; do you want him?" They said: "Of course." My biological mother later found out that my mother had never graduated from college and that my father had never graduated from high school. She refused to sign the final adoption papers. She only relented a few months later when my parents promised that I would someday go to college.

And 17 years later I did go to college. But I naively chose a college that was almost as expensive as Stanford, and all of my working-class parents' savings were being spent on my college tuition. After six months I couldn't see the value in it. I had no idea what I wanted to do with my life and no idea how college was going to help me figure it out. And here I was spending all of the money my parents had saved their entire life. So I decided to drop out and trust that it would all work out OK. It was pretty scary at the time, but looking back it was one of the best decisions I ever made. The minute I dropped out I could stop taking the required classes that didn't interest me, and begin dropping in on the ones that looked interesting.

It wasn't all romantic. I didn't have a dorm room, so I slept on the floor in friends' rooms, I returned Coke bottles for the 5¢ deposits to buy food with, and I would walk the seven miles across town every Sunday night to get one good meal a week at the Hare Krishna temple. I loved it. And much of what I stumbled into by following my curiosity and intuition turned out to be priceless later on. Let me give you one example:

Reed College at that time offered perhaps the best calligraphy instruction in the country. Throughout the campus, every poster, every label on every drawer, was beautifully hand-calligraphed. Because I had dropped out and didn't have to take the normal classes, I decided to take a calligraphy class to learn how to do this. I learned about serif and sans serif typefaces, about varying the amount of space between different letter combinations, about what makes great typography great. It was beautiful, historical, artistically subtle in a way that science can't capture, and I found it fascinating.

None of this had even a hope of any practical application in my life. But 10 years later, when we were designing the first Macintosh computer, it all came back to me. And we designed it all into the Mac. It was the first computer with beautiful typography. If I had never dropped in on that single course in college, the Mac would have never had multiple typefaces or proportionally spaced fonts. And since Windows just copied the Mac, it's likely that no personal computer would have them. If I had never dropped out, I would have never dropped in on this calligraphy class, and personal computers might not have the wonderful typography that they do. Of course, it was impossible to connect the dots looking forward when I was in college. But it was very, very clear looking backward 10 years later.

Again, you can't connect the dots looking forward; you can only connect them looking backward. So you have to trust that the dots will somehow connect in your future. You have to trust in something – your gut, destiny, life, karma, whatever. This approach has never let me down, and it has made all the difference in my life.

My second story is about love and loss.

I was lucky – I found what I loved to do early in life. Woz [Steve Wozniak] and I started Apple in my parents' garage when I was 20. We worked hard, and in 10 years Apple had grown from just the two of us in a garage into a $2 billion company with over 4,000 employees. We had just released our finest creation – the Macintosh – a year earlier, and I had just turned 30. And then I got fired. How can you get fired from a company you started? Well, as Apple grew we hired someone who I thought was very talented to run the company with me and for the first year or so things went well. But then our visions of the future began to diverge and eventually we had a falling-out. When we did, our board of directors sided with him. So at 30 I was out. And very publicly out. What had been the focus of my entire adult life was gone, and it was devastating.

I really didn't know what to do for a few months. I felt that I had let the previous generation of entrepreneurs down – that I had dropped the baton as it was being passed to me. I met with David Packard and Bob Noyce and tried to apologize for screwing up so badly. I was a very public failure, and I even thought about running away from the valley. But something slowly began to dawn on me – I still loved what I did. The turn of events at Apple had not changed that one bit. I had been rejected, but I was still in love. And so I decided to start over. I didn't see it then, but it turned out that getting fired from Apple was the best thing that could have ever happened to me. The heaviness of being successful was replaced by the lightness of being a beginner again, less sure about everything. It freed me to enter one of the most creative periods of my life.

During the next five years, I started a company named NeXT, another company named Pixar, and fell in love with an amazing woman who would become my wife. Pixar went on to create the world's first computer-animated feature film, *Toy Story*, and is now the most successful animation studio in the world. In a remarkable turn of events, Apple bought NeXT, I returned to Apple, and the technology we developed at NeXT is at the heart of Apple's current renaissance. And Laurene and I have a wonderful family together.

I'm pretty sure none of this would have happened if I hadn't been fired from Apple. It was awful-tasting medicine, but I guess the patient needed it. Sometimes life hits you in the head with a brick. Don't lose faith. I'm convinced that the only thing that kept me going was that I loved what I did. You've got to find what you love. And that is as true for your work as it is for your lovers. Your work is going to fill a large part of your life, and the only way to be truly satisfied is to do what you believe is great work. And the only way to do great work is to love what you do. If you haven't found it yet, keep looking. Don't settle. As with all matters of the heart, you'll know when you find it. And, like any great relationship, it just gets better and better as the years roll on. So keep looking until you find it. Don't settle.

My third story is about death.

When I was 17, I read a quote that went something like: "If you live each day as if it was your last, someday you'll most certainly be right." It made an impression on me, and since then, for the past 33 years, I have looked in the mirror every morning and asked myself: "If today were the last day of my life, would I want to do what I am about to do today?" And whenever the answer has been "no" for too many days in a row, I know I need to change something.

Remembering that I'll be dead soon is the most important tool I've ever encountered to help me make the big choices in life. Because almost everything – all external expectations, all pride, all fear of embarrassment or failure – these things just fall away in the face of death, leaving only what is truly important. Remembering that you are going to die is the best way I know to avoid the trap of thinking you have something to lose. You are already naked. There is no reason not to follow your heart.

About a year ago I was diagnosed with cancer. I had a scan at 7.30 in the morning and it clearly showed a tumor on my pancreas. I didn't even know what a pancreas was. The doctors told me this was almost certainly a type of cancer that is incurable and that I should expect to live no longer than three to six months. My doctor advised me to go home and get my affairs in order, which is doctor's code for "prepare to die." It means to try to tell your kids everything you thought you'd have the next 10 years to tell them in just a few months. It means to make sure everything is buttoned up so that it will be as easy as possible for your family. It means to say your goodbyes.

I lived with that diagnosis all day. Later that evening I had a biopsy, where they stuck an endoscope down my throat, through my stomach and into my intestines, put a needle into my pancreas and got a few cells from the tumor. I was sedated, but my wife, who was there, told me that when they viewed the cells under a microscope the doctors started crying because it turned out to be a very rare form of pancreatic cancer that is curable with surgery. I had the surgery and I'm fine now.

This was the closest I've been to facing death, and I hope it's the closest I get for a few more decades. Having lived through it, I can now say this to you with a bit more certainty than when death was a useful, but purely intellectual, concept:

No one wants to die. Even people who want to go to heaven don't want to die to get there. And yet death is the destination we all share. No one has ever escaped it. And that is as it should be, because death is very likely the single best invention of life. It is life's change agent. It clears out the old to make way for the new. Right now the new is you, but someday not too long from now, you will gradually become the old and be cleared away. Sorry to be so dramatic, but it is quite true.

Your time is limited, so don't waste it living someone

else's life. Don't be trapped by dogma – which is living with the results of other people's thinking. Don't let the noise of others' opinions drown out your own inner voice. And, most important, have the courage to follow your heart and intuition. They somehow already know what you truly want to become. Everything else is secondary.

FIFTH INSIGHT

THE MISSION IMPLIES A HIGHER SOURCE

The two most important days in your life are the day you were born and the day you understood why.

Mark Twain

Is choosing a mission a private choice? Or in other words: is this only a private need, to search for meaning and order in a chaotic world, or does everyone in the world "really" have a predetermined role, a destiny, a mission for whose sake they are sent here, and they "only" have to find out what it is and use it?

Most of the philosophical/psychological/coaching approaches, as well as instructional books for finding a mission, find that it's convenient not to deal with this question; it's convenient to be post-modernists and say that everything is in the eyes of the beholder, that if *you* care about something, and if you're eager to do one thing or another — that's a sign that that's where you should be, and that's the "right place" for you. It's convenient to say that *you* are your own indicator. That you know best what is right for you.

Of course, there is truth in these statements, and I also have clarified, in the chapter on talent, what your "right place" is, but in my opinion, you and your desires aren't the only indicator.

Most coaching books and approaches don't deal with the significant question: Is your mission objective or subjective?

Why? Because in order to answer it, we must ask whether there is another partner here, "someone" or "something" who sent you to perform the mission, whether we call it the universe, God, or energy.

In other words, is there an intelligence that is behind the reality that is revealed to us? If we search, will we find a super-director who gives meaning to every point and detail in our individual and general lives?

Most of the books and theorists dealing with the question of destiny "killed" God, leaving man to wallow in his existential emptiness. If so, who, in their opinion, is "guilty" of the fact that we are looking for meaning?

a. The increasing worldwide growth of normative people who are experiencing depression causes a surge in the use of anti-depressants, but also causes people to look for themselves and their happiness.

b. Dissatisfaction with work, with routine, that makes us ask "what do we like/want to do?" instead of the question "How can we earn a living?"

The insight we are discussing now will argue that it's impossible to understand the depth of a mission without putting the Higher Power into the picture. Even though your talents and desires are an extremely important measure, it's impossible to speak of a purpose that stems *only from within you*, only from what makes *you* happy, only from *your* own need to find order in chaos. In this chapter, we would like to argue that the entire world, with all its layers, is pushing us to fulfill the mission.

Therefore, this guide is called "**Who You Were Meant to Be**". Your happiness, that each of you has as an individual, is indeed in itself important in this world, even very important. But that's not the only thing.

This can be seen and understood through the prism of the world of work. Even in an organization of a thousand workers, a happy worker will be a good and efficient worker, who will project his satisfaction inward, to the employees around them, and also outwards, to the customers.

But this happiness isn't an end in itself. We didn't come here just so that you alone should be happy. The happiness of *the whole world* should be important to all of us, that world which can't exist without you, and needs your talent, your uniqueness.

Can a person understand, know what his mission is without relating to Who created him?

The answer is in the affirmative. *There are quite a few "non-believers" who perform their mission faithfully.*

Many personal coaches, psychologists, trainers, and therapists will help you find your purpose even *without discussing* and connecting to the issue of the Higher Power. If so, why did I nevertheless choose to dedicate a chapter in my book to discussing in depth the issue of the Higher Power?

The answer is that the attitude toward the Higher Power isn't a luxury, according to my worldview, but a necessity, Why not? Because Higher Power-consciousness adds two layers to the mission:

a. Commitment to something bigger than me.
b. Integrity/purity of the messenger.

Section A: Commitment to Something Greater than Myself

A combat soldier's ability to deal with difficulties without throwing down his weapon and running away from the battle stems from his beliefs, his world of values.

The belief in the justice of our country's path, the justice of the mission, the understanding that there is no one to save his people instead of him — all these give the soldier tremendous power. But when you're a civilian, not a soldier — what will give you the same power?

My argument is that someone who feels connected to the Higher Power, who believes there is someone above them who runs the world and even "demands" that they fulfill their mission, receives extraordinarily strong power to carry out their mission.

Explanation of Section A: Since you didn't "invent" yourself, you didn't implant skills in yourself, you didn't choose to which father and mother to be born, it would be arrogance to think that you are messengers without a Higher Power, you received a mission without a directing hand granting it. It seems to me that the connection to the Higher Power gives greater authority to the mission than the individual moral obligation of the person who is unsure, who wonders:

Maybe it isn't my destiny?

And maybe only I think I can help?

I met quite a few people in the past, far more talented than myself, who actually don't act/help/assist to the same extent as I do. I asked myself more than once, why is that? After all, they want to help, they believe in themselves and their abilities, they aren't afraid to give; what, then, is missing? The answer is that there is a lack of a greater commitment.

I get up in the morning knowing that if I don't help couples in crisis — who will help them? If they turn to me, the Higher Power sent just me to help them and no one else. My commitment is completely different when, to the consciousness of the work and the mission I engage in, Higher Power-consciousness is added.

And not only that. Higher Power-consciousness commitment creates a clear path, as the Ramchal writes:

It should become clear to the person what his obligation in his world is. That is, the more one understands their duty and for what purpose they have come here, the happier they are. Both in regards to the mission (we have already shown in the previous chapters how much happiness the mission brings to the Higher Power, to the messenger and to the world) and also from the fact that they feel that they are "on the right track," walking on a clear path. Consider how many anxieties are avoided when a person lives in a clear path consciousness, how much confusion, fear, and inner chaos are averted.

If so, pray tell: What is your duty in the world? As fathers, as sons, as sisters, as workers, as managers, wives, as citizens. The fact that you're a CEO, for example, doesn't exempt you from the duty to honor parents. Your mission is impaired if you ignore even one of the layers you're committed to.

Ehud's Poker

Ehud sat opposite me, a knitted skullcap on his head and a gentle smile on his face. He's a cute guy, a yeshiva graduate, married and the father of three, but he looks very shut down, as if there were four hundred tons of sadness "sitting" on him. "Where do you spend most of the day?" I asked. "At the computer," he replied. "I work in SEO, promoting websites." "Nice," I responded with some innocence, "a challenging job, isn't it?" "Well, that's it," he said, and the smile became self-conscious, "I work for a company that promotes poker websites." Of course, I didn't even know about the existence of such sites, and when I raised an eyebrow, he rationalized that despite his qualms, that's what he chose to do, since the big money is in poker sites. "But why?" I insisted, "what's your connection to poker? Why not promote real sites that do something good for society?" "I'll tell you the truth," he said after thinking about it, "I have a job where people don't bother me, which gives me peace of mind, and also, I'm good at it."

"I don't understand," I insisted," eight years of your life god enabled you to study in a yeshiva, you studied *Kamtza* and *Bar-Kamtza* (a Talmudic discussion), Hillel and Shammai (Talmudic Sages), so that afterwards you could waste your talents promoting poker sites? So what if you're 'good at it!' Just see what you look like!"

"You're right," he replied. "I once worked at a company that managed business sites, and indeed I really felt that I was doing something significant. True, I didn't look as exhausted as I do now, but I had too much responsibility. In that job, every week you had to show achievements, to meet goals and high standards. That's not for me," he said decisively.

"It's not such a bright idea to live a life '"under the radar,"' Ehud. True, you yourself are the main loser because of your choices. After all, there is no chance that you will be happy where you are now, promoting poker sites. But you should be aware that you lose at that job also because the whole world loses if that's all you do. It always fits together; an organ detached from the body can't be happy."

Ehud has a wife and three children to support. He couldn't just get up and leave his present job in a moment, but he realized that he couldn't run away from the process of changing jobs. True, he probably likes to think small; he prefers not to take responsibility, and we won't change his temperament, nor do we intend to. But yes, in a year or two, Ehud will have to put himself in a more proper place.

Shira's Ultimatum

About a year ago, a thirty-five-year-old woman, Shira, a lawyer, approached me about a dilemma she's troubled by regarding where she works. She's happy there, everyone likes her very much, and she's successful at what she does. She wants to move up to a more senior position, but the dilemma she posed was that she has been in a relationship for three years, and her partner wants to get married and start a family, and she doesn't really want to. That is, she does want to eventually, but she's not in a rush to do so now; at the moment, her whole world is focused on work. Her partner gave her an ultimatum – we get married or we break up. "What should I do?" she asked me (I know hundreds of women who would love to change places with her, to be faced with such a dilemma, but that's the subject of another book…).

Shira told me that she had been in contact with a personal trainer before she met me, and they told her that she should follow her own yearnings and her own truth, and if her heart is currently in her office, that's where she should be. "If your partner doesn't understand this," her trainer continued, "it's absolutely clear that he isn't inclusive of you and your desires, and as far as you're concerned, it's fine for him to go away."

Do you expect me to say her trainer is wrong? I'm sorry to disappoint you; I'm not going to automatically say that. But in a conversation between us, I perceived that Shira wasn't really happy; the painful truth is that Shira was pretty stifled. "Tell me," I asked her, "how is it that you're so pleased with what's happening at work, and yet you aren't happy?"

Her answer was very precise. "My work is a form of escape," she said, "I'm running away from something, and I don't even know from what." After a few questions, we both understood that Shira was running away from feeling things. We went deeper, on a journey using guided imagery, into the pain and the anger she represses. After an hour she cried like a child (something that hadn't happened to her for several years). Two hours later, she hugged the five-year-old Shira inside of her; after three hours, I felt how something in her body was released; her face and her speech became calm. She came out of our meeting room like a deflated balloon. In our entire conversation, we hadn't said a single word about children and weddings. The next day, she called her partner and said "yes," and that they would be getting married in the summer.

Could it be that the goals I set for myself, on the external, conscious level, are sometimes false ones? You'd be surprised how many people are chasing false goals or missions, and don't understand why they're unhappy.

Section B: Purifying the Messenger/Honesty/Integrity

Inserting the Higher Power into the picture allows you to cleanse the hose thoroughly, to purify the thoughts, desires, speech, and actions of the messenger.

Explanation of Section B: Two doctors can perform a similar, professional mission. However, their internal "purity" level can be different, their motives can be different, and the same is true regarding their level of commitment. In our generation, in order to explain the idea above, we usually use the word *integrity*. Simply put, not all messengers are pure and free from interests.

Unfortunately, reality demonstrates this to us almost every day. We sent highly-regarded and important people to run the state, the police, etc., and what do we find out about them, our messengers? That they aren't honest. One takes bribes, the other abuses, harasses, even rapes the women beneath him, and the third, despite his skullcap and beard, breaks up families. How will this all end?

Want to be loyal messengers? The mission requires of you a thorough cleansing. We are fed up with crooked, dirty messengers.

So yes, even though there are quite a few honest people who perform their mission by virtue of their consciences and morality, with no connection with the Higher Power, I nevertheless wish to claim that the power of the conscience, and the choice of means to carry out the mission, are strengthened when we see the Higher Power before our eyes, who determines for us what it's permissible to do and what it's forbidden for us to do.

Of course, being religious isn't a guarantee that you are honest too — that's obvious, unfortunately — but our discussion isn't about the question of religion, but rather about your attitude toward God, the Higher Power.

There are ultra-Orthodox people who do not believe, and non-religious people who have great faith.

How clean are you? How honest are you? How much do you fake things when no one is looking?

When you put the Higher Power in the picture, a private phone call made by a salaried employee at work is also a kind of "robbery," since your employer pays you, and your time is supposed to be devoted to working for them. Most people will justify themselves with "That's what everyone does, I should be the only sucker who doesn't?"

Now do you understand the role of the commandments? To make you a clean, precise messenger, who doesn't cheat, and doesn't harm anyone else, heaven forbid, whether we're talking about the laws of business or the laws of charity, whether we are talking about the Ten Commandments or signing the *ketubah* (marriage contract). If you are Jewish, you're obligated to fulfill your mission faithfully. Priesthood can't be bought with money, and the rabbinate can't be just about control. You can't behave towards your spouse any way you feel like at that moment, and you can't taste whatever you want to in the supermarket without paying.

Mitzvot between man and his fellow are concerned with the cleanliness of the messenger (the hose towards the garden). *Mitzvot* between man and God deal with the hose's connection to the faucet.

A person can't define integrity according to what the majority does. If most people build themselves up upon the ruins of others — then are we allowed to as well? See what Rabbi Moshe Chaim Luzzatto, the Ramchal, writes in his book *Mesilat Yesharim*: And here we see that even though most people are not openly thieves, that is, by taking their friends' money and putting it in their pocket, nevertheless, *most people get a taste of theft through how they conduct business, and how they rationalize making a profit by causing someone else's loss.*

If so, the knowledge that I am committed to integrity not only on my own behalf, not only on because of the law, not only on behalf of society, and not only in the interest that you love me more, but on behalf of He who created me and sent me here – this knowledge is empowering, and grants me the strength to be *straight in a crooked world*, pure in a dirty world. According to the Sages, when a person reaches heaven, they will be asked a few questions. At the moment we will relate only to the first one: "Did you conduct business faithfully?" That is, have you acted honestly with people financially?

And if I'm not connected to the Higher Power — maybe there's some advice to help me connect?

There is advice that is appropriate, in my humble opinion, both for those whose lifestyle is religious and also for those who don't have a religious way of life: speak to Him. Speak to the Lord out loud. Think about it. I'm like a spy cast into a distant land for a certain mission. There's no chance that I will fulfill my mission without clear instructions, and without constant communication with my Higher Power. I need to update Him on a daily basis about my situation, about what help I need and what I discovered.

Perhaps we'll let the greatest messenger in this field, Rabbi Nachman of Breslov, explain this in his own words:

All the righteous people and the real fearers of God reached their level exclusively by seclusion with the Almighty and by conversing with Him. And especially in these generations, at the end of the exile, when the Evil Inclination is very, very strong, and the generations are very weak in body and soul, it is impossible to be spared from the increased power of the Evil Inclination and the multitude of obstructions, and to approach the Lord, other than through a conversation between a person and their Creator, *to make it a fixed practice to designate a specific time each day to address the Lord*, exclusively in plain language that is to say ,(not in high-flown words, but rather regular speech, as people normally talk to one another), telling the Lord all that is in the person's heart, both to seek forgiveness and pardon for the past, and to beg to be rescued in the future... and even if the person can't speak clearly and explicitly, they can say only a single word, even that is very good, and even if they only say "Master of the Universe"... - that is also very good. Even just preparing for speech, the fact that a person prepares themselves, even though they can't speak, the preparation and desire in themselves are very precious in the eyes of God... Happy is the man who is firm in this, for, whether the person is small or great, it is impossible for them to be a kosher man or woman (and certainly not to be a kosher messenger), other than by means of seclusion with the Almighty and conversation with Him.

(Likutei Moharan B.)

To Sum up the Fifth Insight:

- It's possible to carry out a mission even without "Higher Power-consciousness," but that way the messenger's power and dedication will be less.
- The chapter on merit dealt with the social environment, and the extent to which it strengthens a person in their mission, for enormous powers fill you when so many people say they need you. In this chapter, we discovered another "filling station" that gives a person strength: the connection with the Higher Power. Just as faith can lead a person to do terrible things, so it can, at the same time, help to move mountains for the right thing/to fulfill the mission.
- Messengers are also tested for cleanliness and purity.
- The best advice in order to strengthen the relationship with the Higher Power is: Speak with Him aloud.

Exercise for the Fifth insight: Contact with the Higher Power

The contact with the Higher Power is expressed in different ways in different people. It doesn't matter if the Higher Power, in your eyes, is God or Mother Earth or the Universe, please try to answer these questions. They will help you to fine-tune your relationship with something which is bigger than you:

a. Do you feel "watched" during everyday life? There is someone leading you? Giving directions? Guarding you?

_____

b. Have you ever found yourself praying, turning to heaven?

_____

c. Do you have any feelings for the Supreme Power (even anger, disappointment and conflict are feelings)? If so, what emotion?

_____

_____

_____

d. Have you ever experienced a sense of closeness to yourself or inner enlightenment? When did this happen?

_____

_____

_____

e. Do you ever have the feeling that you're lucky, even though there are areas in which you have difficulty or fail?

_____

_____

f. Do you define yourself as a "believer"? ("religious" defines something else)

_____

_____

g. Assuming you believe there is meaning to everything you're going through as an individual, and that we are going through as a society (if you think that there is no meaning or value to anything, well, you probably wouldn't have stuck with the book until now...) — what do you think is the meaning of your life? Why did the universe "bother" to send You here, to Earth, just now, and make you experience all that you have been through?

_____

_____

AFTER THE FIVE INSIGHTS, WE UNDERSTAND THAT THE MISSION IS A PUZZLE, A PUZZLE COMPOSED OF EVERYTHING A PERSON HAS UNDERGONE IN HIS LIFE. THEREFORE, IN THE FOLLOWING PAGES, WE WILL PRESENT THREE LIFE STORIES, THOSE OF TWO WOMEN AND A MAN, IN ORDER TO INSPIRE YOU IN THE PROCESS OF FINDING YOUR OWN MISSION.

MEETING WITH A SEQUENCE OF EVENTS, WITH UPS AND DOWNS, WITH DILEMMAS, WITH FAILURES, WITH A MISSION THAT BECOMES CLEAR ONLY SLOWLY AND NOT AT ONCE, WILL, I HOPE, HELP YOU TO SCRUTINIZE YOUR PERSONAL STORY WITH NEW GLASSES, AND FIND IN IT THE "HINTS" WHICH WERE PLANTED, OR WHICH APPEARED ON THE WAY, THE CLUES TO THE QUESTION – WHAT IS MY PERSONAL MISSION IN THE WORLD?

SO I WENT TO KFAR SABA TO INTERVIEW SIMONA, TO NETIVOT TO INTERVIEW ESTHER, AND TO MOSHAV NEGOHOT, WHICH IS LOCATED BETWEEN HEBRON AND KIRYAT GAT, TO INTERVIEW ODED.

The Story of a Messenger

THE PENNY DROPPED

I met Simona a few years ago, at one of her life's crossroads, when she was looking for her purpose. We gained some insights, I gave her homework, but the subsequent reality surprised both of us.

Today Simona is fifty-two and feels young and energetic. I first met her when she was fifty, and I asked her, "Is now, when you have three adult children and a few grandchildren, the time to discover your mission?"

Funny, it become clear to me only in retrospect what you were trying to do with me at the time. When we first met, I was in the dark, hiding, regarding my mission.

Only one thing was clear to me all along: I love people, and I want to work with them. I was always looking for a way to help people, to give of myself to others.

At first, I worked as a hairdresser, but that job was interrupted because I got married when I was twenty-four, and we moved to New York.

Just a minute, Simona, go back a little.

My husband Tuvia and I come from extremes, from two opposite worlds: I was an "in", "chic" Tel Aviv girl, everything

in "style," very connected to "what will people say?" I wanted to be at the top of the Who's Who. He was the opposite of me, and that's what I liked about him. I loved that he was a simple man, a kibbutznik. I loved his joy, mostly the joy that emanated from him when he was with his friends. He loved them so much. We got married. We didn't think a lot about it, you know, it's not like things are today.

After the wedding, we moved to America, where I worked in the Syrian-Chalabi community. They're filthy rich Jews, and I was their celebrity hairdresser. I did hair for weddings, and through that, I got to know a lot of people.

In addition, because of my love for cooking, I entertained a lot; but in the middle of all this activity, there was something that always bothered me — seeing single men and women alone, without partners. I caught on to them from miles away, I knew who was single and unattached, and I always tried to connect people, to make a match. I have a keen sense for matchmaking, and a high success rate.

So it sounds like you were doing well.

You have to understand, Moshe, we were at the top. After twenty years in America, you're already settled in. We built a beautiful home and lived a very good life financially. Just to give you an idea, for doing the bride's and her mother's hair, they would pay me between two and three thousand dollars. And they would order a limousine for me, round trip, so that I could get to the event. Do you know a hairdresser who lives like that in Israel? It was something hard to give up. Especially since our children grew up and were also doing well; things were going well for them in America too.

Still, I'm interviewing you in Kfar Saba, not in America.

I don't know how to explain it to you, Moshe. We built a

big house there and finally moved into it. We had a dream come true, but the evening we made a "housewarming," after the guests had left and the children fell asleep, Tuvia asked me, "Are you satisfied?" because he knew from time to time I talked about Israel and I miss it.

And I remember that moment — I had a stunning, sparkling, clean new house, a dream come true, and I answered — "No, I'm not satisfied. I want to make *aliyah*, to move to Israel."

It was an inner voice; I have no way of explaining it. Something in me cried out, "You're not going in the right direction here, you're *really* not going in the right direction here." And Tuvia responded, "Do you want to go back? Ok, we'll go back." As if he's doing me a favor.

I'm a woman to whom my marriage is very important, and with all my desire to return to Israel, if my husband isn't with me 100 percent, I won't go back. I preferred to wait, to let him take his time.

One evening, he brought me an envelope with airline tickets, because we had to go to visit Israel. I reacted with indifference, but he insisted that I open the envelope. It took me some time to realize that the tickets in the envelope were one-way tickets! At that moment, I felt like I had won the lottery.

Was it so simple to return to Israel after twenty years?

Definitely not. I knew that people would try to dissuade me, so I didn't share my plans with any of my friends and customers. Only after the container was loaded and sent off, I invited them to a farewell party. On the day of the flight, I left the house, locked it in tears, and deliberately didn't look back. Before we reached Israel, I had rented a house by telephone, but only when we arrived did we see how terrible it was. In short, getting adjusted in Israel wasn't simple; it was a terrible downfall. Suddenly I realized that I was nothing here, that no one knew me in Israel. And it's better not to talk at all about professional standards and hairdressers' rates.

Ten years have passed since we returned to Israel, and only now I'm keeping my head above water financially.

The great fortune, for me and all of us, is that our "gifts" go with us everywhere, and if you're good at something, then that skill will accompany you wherever you go.

So in Israel too, I got a reputation for high-quality cooking and entertaining, and I opened a gourmet event catering business. Of course, just as I did abroad, I did matchmaking on the side here too.

And then, just when we started managing to keep our heads up financially in Israel, we had a big financial setback, a blow, something to do with the trust we put in people, and in the end, we collapsed, with them, into unbelievable debts.

I remember; you came to me after this incident.

I'm glad you remember, because in the end, with all the crises we went through, including the economic crisis, my awareness of the very idea of the mission sharpened. I realized that money comes and goes, that once I had a lot and now I have nothing, and in the future, I'll have it again, but it really doesn't matter. I remember leaving you with the insight that without people in my life, without the impact that I have on each and every person, I have nothing to do here in this world, I am isolated. If I didn't come here to help people — why did I come here at all?

True, this consciousness was in me before, but not so

strongly. I think this idea opened a door for me, because a few days later, someone phoned me, and called me "the matchmaker."

I remember answering her "Me? A matchmaker? Where did you get that idea?" There are things you do, but you don't catch on in real time. That label was far from me, but suddenly, phones calls started coming. "Tell me, do you have such and such a guy? Do you have such and such a girl?" But the penny hadn't dropped yet.

A week later, Tuvia and I met for a consultation with Rabbi David Ifergan regarding our economic crisis, and as soon as we came in, he told me, "They tell me you're a matchmaker."

"Yes," I told him, "occasionally I make matches." But his approach was different: "They tell me you have to invest all your efforts and all your time in it, and also you have to get paid for it."

True, that's right, there is no reason in the world that you shouldn't make a living from it.

It's amazing that after we left, a flood of phone calls began all at once. You can't imagine, but it was hard for me to take money. In general, it was hard for me to make it "official." When I finally decided to charge a fee, I realized that most of the difficulties are imaginary. I came to the conclusion that if I didn't invest all I had in setting people up, in making matches, my life isn't a life.

I'm glad you're raising the issue of money, because I write about it in my book. This really is an imaginary obstacle for many people on the way to living their mission: to be willing to make a living from what they love and want to do. Some people think you have to make a living only from something you don't like to do. According to what I understand, you decided to take money for matchmaking only after the consultation with Rabbi Ifergan?

Yes, he made me do it.

Charging for your services makes sense. It's not ideal that you help others, and yet be poor and needy yourself; that's not the idea. So wait, let me understand, you take money from someone at the start, when they sign up and register, and then you start working with them? How much money?

It started at $150 and now the rate has gone up to a $200 registration fee. It's not limited in time; I mean to say, even if I have to be by your side for two or three years, that's the sum, until the wedding. And if my matchmaking services end in a wedding, the payment is $1500.

The question is different. The question is: Why, when you made meals for people and styled their hair, it was easy for you to take money, and here you had a hard time?

I found it hard to do when catering too. I think it's a matter of excessive self-nullification.

In my book, I call this phenomenon "false humility." In practice, today, thanks to the fact that you charge money, you work a lot more on matchmaking, and don't just do it "on the side."

Rabbi Ifergan told me, "If you won't take money, don't make matches." And right after I left the rabbi I had a meeting with a single guy. I trembled, my life, like I was on a fateful date, I felt the sweat pouring down my back.

And what went through your mind?

That I prefer to work twenty hours rather than deal with charging money. And at the end of the meeting when we reached the payment stage, the bachelor guy told me, "Ok,

no problem. Here, take it." I didn't believe it, that's all there is to it? It's so simple?

And now it's easy for you to collect money?

It's still not effortless. The subject of money is always on my mind. I have thoughts: maybe I won't take it now, maybe later, let's talk about it later on. And then I force myself: No! No! No! Talk about it now!

You don't want to register and pay? You don't have to. Thank you and goodbye. Still, the inflexibility of the subject, having to be firm about money, costs me dearly emotionally.

But today, when I deal with this feeling less and less, a place opens up inside me, and I have the internal energy needed to be a "sniffer dog," to be precise in matchmaking, to plumb the depth of each and every one, to ignore the clothes, to ignore the outer shells.

There is a matchmaker who, since her success in the eighties, is very famous, a household name in Israeli terms, I even remember her from my childhood. Not long ago she called me and we met. Actually, it's more accurate to say I joined a meeting with her client, and suddenly I saw to my great surprise that she charges $9000 to register, and nevertheless loads of people come to her.

And you know what? After seeing her in action, I can tell you, without conceit or lack of modesty, that I work better than she does. She's professional and experienced, but my instincts are better. I told her I'd probably be her heiress.

How many hours a day do you invest?

Lots. I fall asleep and wake up with matchmaking. Really. They call me at midnight. Ask people on the street what does a matchmaker do? They'll tell you she phones him and phones her and the story is over, you two work things out yourselves. But it doesn't work that way.

I'm like a mother + a girlfriend + a psychologist. I talk, I include, I advise based on my experience; after all, I could be the mother of most of the guys and most of the girls. And believe me, you don't know how much they suffer, they're really miserable. My heart goes out to them. It's not easy in our generation.

Look, Moshe, you too, when you want to deliver a good lecture, you learn the subject in depth, and then you try to convey it in such a way that you feel that you have made an impact on people, that you have helped them, that you have reached them, that they got the message. Sometimes I also hear myself talking to people, and even if nothing came of the date I sent them on, I feel that I helped them, that the talk we had moved them a step forward on the path to a relationship. It fills me with joy.

Today, I understand that I have to be whole with myself, I have to release what should be released. Once, if a date didn't work out, I would feel guilty. Today I understand that that isn't my role. Only the effort is mine.

On the one hand, you can't take responsibility for someone else's life. On the other hand, I see how many people need this help that I offer, this guidance.

Wait a minute, do you advertise to get people to come to you? Do you have a website? Facebook?

I don't advertise. I'm lousy at marketing, and the internet is a foreign language to me; I hate it. I don't even have a business card, and still, people call. My name gets around by word of mouth.

I don't understand, so how do you show pictures?

I don't show pictures. It's not a meat market. When clients

see a picture, no matter what I say, they reject the person in a second. Everything is externality. That's not for me, Moshe, that's not my credo.

You're a real "voice calling in the wilderness," that's not a common approach.

And you probably think that my guys and girls are in the computer in Excel tables, right? And that I have some kind of software that cross-tabulates the data? I'll surprise you. Everything is on paper. I'm not a computer person; everything is in binders.

Simona shows me her binders and I'm amazed; if she doesn't use software to match up her clients, she must have a matchmaking system inside her head. "Tell me," I asked her, "one of the complaints I hear quite a bit about matchmakers is that you tell them what you're looking for, and then they try to pressure you to go out with a guy or a girl about whom you said explicitly that there's no match. Are you different in this area, too?"

There are dating advisors for whom the match works like this: "Are you breathing? Do you have a pulse? Great, then get married." Do you know why something like that happens to those matchmakers? Because they have feelings of guilt, because sometimes they didn't get the client out for a date for a long time, so they get them to go out with someone not suitable, just to say that they did their duty.

Therefore, in the first meeting a client, I declare in advance: I don't work by the clock, I don't know when the penny will drop in my head for you. Sometimes a girl will call and ask "You haven't set me up for a while; don't you have someone in your files for me?" Of course, I've got all kinds of people there, but I don't just pick anyone; it doesn't work that way. When I feel something is right and my intuition tells me to go forward, I try to make a connection. I'm not a computer. My intuition guides me in matchmaking.

You yourself told me then, when I met you regarding my mission, "Go on your own pathway, perform your mission faithfully, with all your heart, and the results will come by themselves; and in any event, the results also don't depend just on you." That's what I do, and that's why most of the time I'm accurate; every date is exact, I don't go through the motions, just to do my duty.

One night when I was half asleep, I suddenly thought of a twenty-three-year-old girl, and at the same time a twenty-four-year-old guy came to mind, both of whom, of course, I know from my pool of prospects. First thing in the morning I called the young man and told him, "Listen, congratulations, I found you a bride." He began to interrogate me, "Who is she? What does she look like?" I stopped him and said: "You're not going to get anything about her out of me — no information. The penny dropped in my head about you two, and that's it. You have to meet her. She's stunning. That's all."

Then I called her, and she also started in with interrogations: "Who is he? Where is he on Facebook?" I told her, "You won't get anything out of me. You'll be crazy about him, and not just you, your mother will be crazy about him too." I invited them here, to my house, and prepared a romantic meal for them. You have no idea how much they're in love. They got married before I could sneeze.

Some people call me. "Well, I signed up with you three months ago and nothing happened," and I explain that it's a process, that we're in the middle of a process, a mental and emotional process in which you need to get new insights and

throw out old ones that don't move you forward.

Wow, you need a lot of patience to be a matchmaker. It's like psychological therapy.

Do you realize that many of them are in distress? In difficulty? In confusion?

Yes, I do, but still, even today, in addition to matchmaking, you continue with catering and hairstyling. In the book I'm writing, I ask a question: "What does a person who has a lot of skills and desires to help do, how do they know it's one thing and not the other? How do they know what to invest their time and energy in?"

I realized that although I really enjoyed preparing food for people, that that wasn't my mission, because I see my success in matchmaking. I see the distress people feel, I feel that my clients really suffer, as if from a Heavenly decree or a plague. I can't ignore it. There, in catering, I feed the body, and here, in matchmaking, I feed the soul; I save a person from loneliness.

In exactly the same way the lessons you give, Moshe, enliven my soul, I want to do the same thing and help others too. I don't know how to lecture like you, so I assist on the spiritual level here, in matchmaking. Food can also be made spiritually, but when I cater, only I'm there, in the kitchen, in designing the event, in the hospitality. The spirituality I find in food is only through my own personal intentions; it doesn't involve other people. Matchmaking is different.

When someone who knows me from America comes to Israel and asks me to do her hair, I earn in two hours about two times as much as I earn at matchmaking in a whole month! There is no comparison at all.

But I don't feel a mission in catering or hairdressing.

These are respectable jobs that provide a livelihood, and perhaps they are someone else's mission, but for me, they aren't. Nothing gives my soul a fresh breath of air like matchmaking.

Rabbis approach me to make matches for their children. I say to myself "Me? Who am I anyway?" But yes, it seems they're right; I'm the one to do the job.

When one of my clients, a guy or a girl, gets married, I light up. I'm dazzled. I go around lit up for a month. But sometimes a date I set up isn't just for the wedding at the end. Sometimes I have to help the guy or girl back into dating; "their soul is extinguished" because of previous bad dates, because of some insult they experienced, and they stopped going out. A twenty-five-year-old girl who hadn't dated for three years came to me. How does such a thing happen? She must have had some *really* bad dates.

So I got her out of her mess; what I did was really a kind of therapy treatment. I sent her on a date with the absolute knowledge that the guy didn't fit her and that they'd never get married. But, on the other hand, who was the guy I got her a date with? Someone I know she'll have a good time with, she'll have a positive experience, so she'll see that there are good men, and something will soften up within her after all the bad years. This date will put her on the path to marry someone else in the end. It even may not be someone I introduced her to, but it doesn't matter, I know I helped her, that I was a step in her path to marriage.

Just a "step in her path" isn't something you can brag about; what matters in your profession is just weddings, isn't that so?

I don't measure myself just by how many weddings I made. A matchmaker's role has so much mission in it. Each one of my clients has their own individual next stage. For some, the next stage isn't a wedding; even so, when I move them there, I fulfill my mission. The more I give, the more my own batteries get charged up. I get the energy I need to continue.

A man of sixty-eight, divorced four times, came to me. I looked at him and said to myself, "Wow, great, what optimism." A year ago I would have said, "How can I help him after four times? He's probably a lost case." Thank God, I work based on my judgment; it's not easy, but yes, he is sixty-eight years old and I understand that for him, marriage is a goal. His worldview is: You don't give up until you find. I admired him for it.

You ask about my other skills? I combine skills. I invite my clients to eat with me, and they melt away. I open their hearts with atmosphere and Moroccan cooking... and not only! If, for example, there's a lady who's not very glamorous, I do her hair. Let her go on a first date feeling good about herself. In short, I combine skills.

Another thing I talk about in the book are failures, which are also necessary for a mission. What's your "failure" in relationships? From what I know, you have an awesome husband and an awesome marriage; you married at a young age. What are your sore points?

When I was a month old my parents divorced. It was in Morocco, and immediately afterward, we, the whole family, moved to Israel without him. That means I grew up without a father. As a girl, I never saw a good marriage, normal parenthood, a normal man. My mother didn't remain alone. After ten years, my mother married again, but then divorced again. I didn't grow up with a model for healthy relationships. Probably because of that, to this day, when I enter the homes of couples who don't get along, I sense it right away.

On the other hand, or on the same hand, depending on how you look at it, I fought for my marriage. I did everything I could to make it succeed. There were a lot of issues between us, because Tuvia and I want different things. We're made of different materials, which is both good, and also difficult and frustrating. I realized very quickly that he isn't my twin in terms of hobbies and activities, but my *tikkun*, my correction, my repair. I realized that I should never expect that he and I would have similar desires and thoughts.

Once a guy came to me. I asked him to tell me about himself. He said, "Me, I love dancing, and I'm looking for someone who likes to dance too." I don't understand this approach, my husband loves football, so I also have to love football? I like to cook — he has to like it too?

So you feel there is a connection between your pain regarding other people's relationships and the childhood you experienced? You yourself didn't need a matchmaker, but fundamentally, you saw relationships as something difficult, lonely.

I never looked at relationships that way. But I did understand that there was no other way, that there is no way I would live alone, that growing up without a father isn't an option. And living without a husband, with all the difficulties, isn't an option either.

Could it be that I have closed off this emotional place in childhood? That I repressed things? I don't know — I don't remember much about my childhood.

My father moved to Israel ten years after us. He lives in up North. Technically, we're family, but I have no feelings for him. When we meet at family events, the whole environment is stressed-out because of me, the outsider. Do I feel comfortable? Actually, I don't feel anything, neither anger nor affection. He is a complete stranger as far as I'm concerned, and so, the feeling of abandonment stays with me. Every time you experience something, that something is seared into you, even if it's only material abandonment, like when we left America. Then, when we left, I was afraid of abandonment, of instability.

You know what, Simona? While you're talking, I understand something else. You don't come from a religious home, but rather from a traditional one. Both in Israel and in the United States, you encountered multi-faceted Judaism. I think that this encounter also influenced you on your mission. You know why? Because I don't know many matchmakers on whose lists can be found the ultra-Orthodox, the religious, and also the secular. Most matchmakers focus on one sector. How do you manage to make this connection?

I love people and don't look at the outer mask or the definitions which limit them. Breslov *Hasidim* can only marry Breslov *Hasidim*? Lubavitchers can only marry *Lubavitchers*? I don't close doors; what difference does it make if you're secular or religious? Everyone needs help. I have no doubts on this subject; I go with my truth.

Look, one day the penny dropped in my head about a girl who is not religious; she's a little interested in studying Judaism here and there, but she's not religious, she doesn't observe the Sabbath or anything else. The point is that on the male side, the penny dropped about someone who is a rabbi. A real rabbi, someone who completed rabbinical studies, who teaches in a yeshiva. I sent her to hear a Torah lesson which he gives before I sent them out on a date. She told me I was crazy, and that there was no way that that would work.

That I'm "unreal," in her words, to even raise it as an option. Not because of him personally, she said, but because of the gaps between us, of course.

A week later I out-maneuvered her. I told her I wanted to introduce him to someone else; I just want to make sure her answer is final and that he's not for her. Suddenly, she spoke differently: "Give me time to think…," and so on. Indeed, they went out for a few weeks. From conversations with her, I understood that he didn't understand what a woman is, and how to behave toward one, so I grabbed him for a talk. I shouted at him that just to know the Talmud by heart is no big deal, there are other things you have to know, and I gave him tips, real "do and don'ts" with girls. In short, he progressed a lot; he was a good guy; he understood his mistakes and improved by leaps and bounds.

However, after a few weeks, there was a flare-up. He called me on the phone to ask what to do because she's angry with him, and she sent me a message at the same time that she intends to break up with him. What should I do? Give up? But I know they'd be good together, they're still dealing with peeling off the first layers of the differences between them, and he's someone that you can work with. He learns, and he applies what he learns; that's not something to take for granted. Women think that they should look for a finished product, but there's no such thing. You have to work on every man. You have to work at a relationship.

I sent him a message — "Propose." He was in shock. "Are you crazy?" he asked "She's mad at me!" I wrote him again — "Propose," and I shut off my cell phone so that they couldn't call me.

He proposed while she wanted to break up with him —

can you believe it? And she agreed, and they got married! A rabbi and a not religious girl. And you can't imagine how happy they are.

What a story, Simona! You do play around with the truth, and it seems to me you can also fall on your face in such cases, but the story is amazing.

I don't lie. Definitely not. If I say he's cute, he's cute. If I say he's stunning, he's stunning. I don't lie.

True, you may need to move some chess pieces around to make a pair come together — so why not? Should you let the title "rabbi" interfere with them getting married? It's permissible to lie a little to help relationships, but I want you to know that I'm just the opposite of a liar; I tell people the poignant truth.

Like for instance?

A rich Jewish fellow from Switzerland came to me. "How much do you take for a wedding?" "$1,500," I said. He offered to pay me ten times that amount — $15,000 — if I would take care of him first. I didn't agree. Everybody counts. I told him that, too. Wait like everyone else, until the penny drops. I'll be damned if he thinks that afterwards he'll buy his wife with money too.

A guy with crooked teeth once came to me and asked to marry a model.

"What are you looking for?"

"Someone beautiful."

"What else?"

"Beautiful."

"What else?"

"Beautiful."

"Tell me," I asked him, "why do you only want someone

perfect? Are you perfect? Are your teeth perfect?" He went and had his teeth straightened, and then came back to me after a while. And what do you think, that I gave in to him? When he came back with his teeth straight, I asked him: "And what about your conceit?"

You're funny, Simona. You remind me of a story about someone whom the matchmaker told, after a few attempts, that he was too conceited, and to work on his pride. A year later, the guy returned and thanked the matchmaker for the advice. "I've been working all year just on my pride, now I'm really humble," he said, "now can you introduce me to girls?"

"It's great you came," the matchmaker said, "there's someone I introduced you to then, a year ago, and you weren't interested, but I really think you're right for each other, maybe you'll check it out again? Who knows?"

The guy answered: "If I didn't want her when I was conceited, why would I want her now that I'm really humble?"

That's a great story. I have more crazy stories, want to hear?
Sure.

A fifty-year-old man came to me and wanted a thirty-year-old girl. Not over thirty. Twenty-five or twenty-six is the best, he said.

Then he said to me, "I want her really slim." I said to him, "No problem, we'll ask her to fast, so by the time you go out, she'll be really thin."

A girl told me about the boy I sent her on a date with: "He's amazing, he's the man of my dreams," she couldn't praise him highly enough — and then she said to me, in all seriousness, "Do you have the same thing, only taller?

I told her I have a production line, and so I would order one for her, if she would just give me the precise measurements.

No, Simona, enough, stop here, indeed you're making me and the readers laugh, but you should put these stories in the book *you* write about matchmaking! Finally, Simona, do you want to tell me about your dream about your mission? Where are you in four or five years?

I dream of opening a matchmaking agency that lots of people will come to. An agency with secretaries, and matchmakers that I train.

If I was chosen to do this mission, then why not make it big, right? Do you know how many people need help in this area? I won't rest until everyone has a partner. As the Bible says "It's not good for man to be alone."

The Story of a Messenger Who is Not Good at Anything

I went to interview Esther Lachman, thirty-three years old, married and mother of four, who lives on Moshav Shuva near Netivot. Esther is the founder of Arugot Cosmetics, a family boutique workshop for the development and manufacture of organic natural cosmetics, and she is the author of "*Natural Pharmacy*."

I met Esther through my wife, who was very attracted to her Facebook posts, and who began ordering products from her; she purchased Esther's book from her, and enrolled in a course under her guidance: "Plants for Life."

I was interested in interviewing someone who told me that her mission expressed her talents and creative powers.

I thought Esther could inspire many women.

Tell me a bit, Esther, about your life. Where did you grow up and learn, where do you come from?

I was born in Kfar Etzion in Gush Etzion, a religious kibbutz of knitted *kippah* wearers. My parents were a little different from most of our neighbors. My mother was born and lived in England, my father in the United States, and we were a bit untypical kibbutz members. I always felt that we were different, starting with the language we spoke at home,

mainly English, and on through the fact that although my parents were officially kibbutz members, on paper, they didn't fully accept the template of the kibbutz, "the box."

Today, when I look back on things, I feel that that differentness was a gift, even if I felt I was an outsider then, when they looked at me strangely and made statements which I'll never forget, such as "What, you're not Israeli pioneers, your grandfather didn't die on this land?"

In high school, I joined the youth groups in Sde Boker, in the Negev desert. When I went out into the desert, I felt that I had come home, that the desert is my place. Before the army, I did a year of national service in Sde Boker as a tour guide, and in the army, I returned to Sde Boker as a teacher. Later, I worked in the Be'er Sheva prison as a teacher of Judaism and art; and later on, I did that in Yeruham too. In fact, in those years, I abandoned religious practice and the religious world as I perceived it then. Today I understand that I only left the outer shell of religion. Maybe you'll censor this part out? It sounds like a criticism of Judaism...

Why censor it out? Just when your story was getting interesting...

As a child and as a teenager, I felt that people on the kibbutz were dealing with unnecessary things, as far as I was concerned, such as girls' sleeve length, and whether or not married women should modestly cover their hair, but they weren't dealing with the heart of Judaism. In my opinion, religion to them was a communal activity that everybody participated in, everyone did the same thing, but there were no questions asked about the inner essence of Judaism.

At Sde Boker, I discovered principled, values-based secularism, which was, as I saw things then, deeper. I met secular people who burrow within their souls, who go out to the desert, and after the army, I moved to the cliff of kibbutz Sde Boker for almost a year. As far as I was concerned, that was my home.

My soul went out to nature and, following nature, to different people, and I made treks to places that preserved ancient handicrafts. I was interested in finding villages and people who live traditionally, so I started flying and traveling to all kinds of countries: in Europe, the United States, India, Jordan, the Sinai, Malta, Georgia, Bulgaria, Hungary, England, and Scotland.

Some of these trips were made to track down traditional craftsmen. I would find a woman weaving and spinning wool, and I would live with her and learn her art.

Really?

Yes. And my gauge was Coca-Cola. If they didn't sell Coca-Cola somewhere, then I could be there. For me, Coca-Cola reflected how far Western civilization had penetrated. I searched for different lifestyles, for untainted places. I remember walking with my husband and arriving at a village in India; remote isn't the word. I was very sick, and I can't forget how, just as I lifted my head from the rickshaw, the first thing I saw was a gigantic graffiti of Coca-Cola on the only wall standing in this village. Just for your information: They don't have running water in the village, but Coca-Cola was there. As far as I was concerned, that lit up a red light.

You were very sick? What happened?

We'll get to it soon. On my trips I understood that in all these places, which we call "backwaters," there are several things in common:

a. They have a different rhythm of life, one that is usually associated with ancient crafts.

b. The local people's way of life also consists of a connection with the soil and plants; that is to say, the people who used herbs usually also grew them themselves, unlike the Western herbs we buy, like miniature mushrooms or a gold heart flower from China. In more traditional places, this is part of the connection to the land, not some kind of hobby or a luxury to do in your spare time; they need these plants as part of their life. Do you want to be able to treat your son's ear infection? Or your husband's finger, which was injured in the field? Or a new-born baby? You must have plants, the spices and herbs that every child there is familiar with.

In the course of the trips abroad I told you about, I met Itai, my husband. When we met, he was a member of an international organization of Palestinians and Jews; he was an idealistic leftist, and at the same time, he was beginning to return to religious observance. I remember telling him: "You can check out the subject of religion, take a spin and come back, but I'm done. I was there, I was religious, and I know what it is. Right now you're excited about the prayer book and prayer, but it will pass, you'll get over it soon."

Of course, he didn't understand what I was talking about, and he asked me to just study together with him. I agreed. Together we studied the book *Likutei Moharan* by Rabbi Nachman of Breslov, and I felt that he, Rabbi Nachman, and Itai as well, were presenting Judaism to me from another direction, one which was like nothing I knew in childhood, and that this Judaism, the piety, the inner speech, was the most relevant, fascinating, interesting and binding thing there is. I felt that for me, it was like coming to a spring. When I would come to a spring I always looked for the place the water gushes forth from, the emanation; that's where you feel the power of the spring. That's exactly how I felt about learning Rabbi Nachman's words with Itai.

After we got married, we went on a mission to India on behalf of the Jewish Agency, exactly two weeks after our wedding. It was the mistake of our lives. We weren't like Israelis who go on treks to India as a trip; we actually *lived* in Bombay and Goa, but I got very sick there. We tried to travel and recover, but we failed, and we returned, crushed, to Israel.

What does "sick" mean? What happened?

We arrived in India during the monsoon period, and in the "pigsties" we lived in, there was a serious sanitary problem. I got a stomach infection, and I was admitted to a hospital, but the hospitals in India are themselves unhygienic.

Itai took care of me and nursed me. We had just gotten married; this was a most unromantic situation for a couple who just got married. But my condition wasn't just "unromantic," but really life-threatening. I was on the verge of death three times. When we returned to Israel, I felt that I had gone through a kind of shake-up, as extreme conditions tend to affect us. They bring us to the edge and raise questions. When we returned to Israel, we were told that we couldn't get pregnant. My health was very precarious, and the doctors thought I couldn't get pregnant.

Wow, that's not trivial news.

Definitely not. But something good happened during this period. Slowly, I recalled all the places I had been in, the villages, the way of life, the ancient medicine. And, like a spark, I would remember all the "desert hours" I had put in. As a result, I put together a different way of looking at things, a critical look at the culture in which we live. I thought that if we, as a family, won't be vigilant, we would find ourselves slowly sliding into a capitalistic, comfortable lifestyle.

We lived at the yeshiva; my husband studied Torah, and there was community life. I felt that I could be attached to life, that is, aware and conscious, both in *bad times*, in sickness, in extreme circumstances, and in *good times*, such as I had had in the desert, but that the connection I felt there was slipping through my fingers in ordinary life, in my routine, everyday life. And then, precisely from within my illness, I felt that medicinal plants are a kind of bridge that brings some benefits:

a. A simple connection to everything that lives and gives life, with a powerful life force that exists around us, even in the garden.

b. A change of thinking about life in Western culture. From the age of zero, we are taught that responsibility for health, for sanity, whatever, is in the hands of experts. Wherever I teach, they ask me: What did you study, and where? What documents do you have? I do have diplomas, but the simple answer is that life teaches us, each day and every moment. I felt the connection to plants gave me balance.

Here in Israel we are "as if" in the Land of Israel and live our lives "as if" we are there, but the truth is that we are bathed in cultures that seep through to the most basic things. A doctor tells a woman who just got married that she can't conceive? If I were a "good girl," I would uncritically accept the doctor's advice and make peace with this decree, but I feel that the command "and you shall choose life" is what which made me not listen to the doctor's advice.

Your book is about finding a destiny, isn't it? We always laugh about this, that if you want to reach your destination, just turn on Waze, because it says: "You have reached your destination." Right? "You have reached your destination." As if there's exactly one place you have to arrive at, and you're actually in some kind of competition all throughout your life to reach it. But in Hebrew, your goal is *destiny*, not *destination*. Continual present. Getting to be an herbal therapist is a destination, but destiny, in my eyes, is something that changes from moment to moment. Now my mission is to learn to live as a couple, and tomorrow my mission is to learn to raise children, and in the afternoons to prepare *dreidels* (spin top toys) with the children, and at this very moment my calling is to sit with you and to be interviewed.

To live my destiny, I have to consent, internally, to participate fully in life. This life of ours is served to us on a silver platter. I look at people who are "searching for themselves," and I feel the search should be easy, that everything is spread out right before them.

The power to choose is the strongest force, the richness of the world is literally spread out before you, take it into your health, into your daily decisions: What do I put into my mouth? What health do I want? What medicine do I consume? How do I educate my children? What kind of relationship do I want? And more. The choice is mine.

So this terrible disease brought you not only life, but the

ability to bring a good and healthy life to others. But most likely the path between the decision to connect with the help of medicinal herbs, and the stage where you yourself manufacture the so-called Arugot line of products, wasn't so simple.

Right. Things don't happen like in the movies, where you get a sudden insight or a lightbulb lights up that says that there should be a cosmetics company or a school for medicinal plants. Rather, it's a process that is born slowly from the circumstances of life.

Itai had another business, and at that time I learned per-maculture with Talia Schneider, a method of environmen-tal planning and an ecological way of life. At the same time, I wanted to engage in something I like, and which would bring us in some cash on the side. Following permaculture, we started growing our own vegetables, raising chickens, goats; we explored independent life's limits: To what extent can someone sustain themselves, independent of external systems?

The climax was when I was pregnant with our first son, when I read the labels on the products we bought at the pharmacy, and was exposed to the "chemical soup" which is in the conventional products sold to us in stores, which contain hidden byproducts of industrial plants, and mate-rials that damage the body, all in a beautiful wrapping. It seemed horrifying and abnormal to me. I began to concoct homemade products for the infant who was soon to be born, and after he was born, for the children who came after him. And here and there I saw that what in our small family was self-evident — for example, the diaper cream we made from flowers we raised in the garden — to others didn't seem so obvious at all. Suddenly, two neighbors also wanted the

cream, and then other neighbors too. The business simply grew on its own; it grew from the bottom up completely. To this day, we feel that we are responding to reality, we are really going with the signs we are shown.

It's nice that your neighbors ask for your products... but then what?

It wasn't as if we had some vision in mind and we went in that direction, but in fact, we did respond to reality, because at some point those using our products changed from neighbors to customers. I used to prepare everything in our home kitchen, until we felt that the work was getting too mixed into the house, and we moved the manufacturing process to a wooden cabin that was attached to the house. Demand increased, and then we received a grant from one of the offices of the Negev-Galilee Development Ministry, which supports businesses in the south of Israel, and we moved production to one of the houses in the moshav. From there, the business meandered to a store in Netivot, and now it's in a factory.

At that point, we realized that the products were just an excuse for us to pass on a kind of worldview and a way of life, one that seems obvious and simple to us, to many people for whom it's something innovative, and a gift.

I don't know what to call this phenomenon. Is this the natural way, or connection to oneness? To me, it's all one thing. If a person knows himself, creation, nature, he or she can also connect to the Creator of this creation. There is an emanation in each person which is positive, natural, and when the person begins to remove wrappings and discover it, it becomes exposed and awakes by itself. There is no need to convince people about religious observance, rather, help them return to themselves, to their emanation.

We opened a school for herbal medicine and natural pharmacy. In the workshops we presented, we see that people begin to deal with nature and come here, and see us living like this, and the puzzle began to be put together by itself. You don't have to talk to anyone too directly; "the whole is greater than the sum of its parts." I just bring in a piece of turmeric, for example, and talk about how this piece can replace the antibiotics in your house, and suddenly the person realizes that they no longer have to run to the doctor for every silly thing. It creates some internal discourse in them, I hope, some new dynamic in the house.

We're talking about a short course, a total of eight sessions, and women say it changed their whole home, and it moved them closer to themselves and their children. Suddenly, aside from yelling at the children and cleaning up the house and doing chores, they find the time for a daily massage for their child. I feel that I've been privileged to open a window through which you can look at the world a little differently.

It really is a window, a very special window.

To me, something about this process already started during childhood on the kibbutz. From a young age, I walked around with a feeling that we in our family are different, no matter what we do. In communal eating area, my parents would embarrass me when they spoke to one another in English; at some point, I resigned myself to this situation and said to myself, "Okay, you're not like everyone else, so go on. Go on your own path." From the beginning, I wasn't in the same footrace as everybody else. My parents were different, they behaved differently, they didn't catch on. Even in religious matters, I remember my mother asking me in the summer,

"Why don't you walk around just in a tank top and shorts?" In England, a Jew can be a Sabbath observer and then go to the beach, be very exposed. Definitions of "religious" and "secular" are more flexible for Jews there.

I had a strong feeling, one that accompanied me all along, that I was *already* outside the box. "Now go exploring the beautiful wide open spaces of this world," I told myself.

I feel that I have received a gift for life in the form of this differentness, because it has helped me to put together my own path.

Well, of course. If you won't be yourself, what will you be? Someone else's chemical soup?

You remind me now of the story of Rabbi Zusha. This is a story that has always been with me. Rabbi Zusha told his students that when he goes up to heaven, they won't ask him "Why weren't you Avraham Avinu (our father Abraham)?" but rather, "Why weren't you Zusha?" And I really do feel that every human being comes to this world with a certain shade of color, and with a gift that can be born only through that person's own vessel. Unfortunately, we so easily join the mainstream, the central and boring stream. We take things for granted.

When I was little, I made trouble for my parents. In school, they yelled at me, "Why do you always ask 'who said so?'" "Sit quietly!" "Do what you're supposed to do." Today, when I give lectures, I feel that the question "Who said so?" is the most important question. Why do you accept certain basic assumptions so easily? Why do you think that that's the only path to healing, or to health, or to nutrition, or to educating children?

I very much hope I will be worthy of it, but I really feel

that what we will be asked in heaven is: "Where is your shade of color? Why don't we see it down there, in the physical world? Why doesn't it shine?"

The last course I gave was attended by nurses from a sick fund (HMO), a department manager, and two conventional pharmacists. They realized very quickly that theirs wasn't the proper way. Now they say that they are ashamed to give people drugs, when they know exactly what they contain. We know who finances the drug studies, we know how the system works, and the alternative is so simple and available, and it's here.

The truth hurts but must be said: This isn't the gift you should bring to the world, selling the drugs of a pharmaceutical company. Why did you choose this job, pharmacy? Because you had a desire to give, a desire to help people, to deal with healing, isn't that so?

Maimonides said that a drug that helps one organ and damages another organ can never be called "medicine."

Right. That's why it bothers me. Isn't enough injustice done all over the world by medicine that doesn't exactly heal, but that only infects you with chemicals and side-effects, that only creates an addiction to drugs – should we ourselves also do injustice personally, ourselves? If you came to bring healing to the world, find out what shade of color your healing is, and what the special thing is that only *you* can give to this world. I don't know why, but our culture is full of fear. Fear to dare, to be different, to do what *you* think is right.

Tell me, Esther, I have to ask this question: Despite what you said about how every moment you perform your mission, etc., my feeling as a man is that it's easier for me to go outside and do great things than it is for you. I have someone who takes the burden away, who helps me, who clears things away for me and takes burdens away from me. For the women in our world, there's no that doubt going out and doing great things is complicated. How did you experience your mission from a feminine viewpoint, especially with four small children?

That's true, even though the serious spike of Arugot was made six years ago, exactly at the moment our first son was born. Four children, very close births, and we are flourishing.

I feel that every child brought a gift with them. The first one brought us Arugot, and the second brought my writing with her — I suddenly began writing to the newspapers, for magazines, something I hadn't done before. My children and my family constantly sharpen me.

I think you're right in another aspect. My husband and I are different in our perception of the mission. I think part of the mission also includes sleeping well and eating well and living well, in simplicity, in utmost simplicity. This really is the course that guides me. Men have a broad mindset and a desire to do a mission with devotion, self-sacrifice (literally, in Hebrew, *soul-sacrifice*).

Esther smiles her sweet smile and looks at my wife, as if to speculate that she's the one whom she'll get confirmation from, a sort of sisterhood, while I will identify with her husband.

I don't sacrifice my soul, it's precious to me. I create a small kingdom. A small plot of God here in this world, with my children.

I see that with men it's about conquering, big time — establishing an empire. And I say to Itai, "Forget it, I want small." For example, we had some teachers in our school who taught all over the country; I asked Itai to come down from this high horse, from the "empire" — we should keep

our operation local. If it's important for someone to learn natural pharmacology, they will come here, to Netivot. I'm very connected to Netivot, which is located in just a corner of the world, and there is something sweet here, sane and simple; every time I go to teach in Tel Aviv or Herzliya, everything there is in high gear, overdrive. Tel Aviv makes me dizzy.

So women want a small empire?

Women want every day as it comes, unplanned. Maybe I'm talking in the name of all women a little, and surely we can't generalize, so I'll talk about myself. There were as many business plans for us as there are grains of sand on the beach, but a business plan graph looks like a graph of an earthquake to me. I don't connect with it.

Another example: just when someone who wanted to join us as a business partner came around, I became pregnant and disappeared for four months. It seems to me that the feminine place is simply to relate to things on a day-to-day basis.

Our workers already know: When I am with the children, as far as I'm concerned, Arugot doesn't exist: no phone calls, no emails. I was with the children in the garden now, carving *dreidel* toys. I feel that when I manage to grasp the present, to be in the present with my family, then when I later get to Arugot, I suddenly have quiet, a breath of energy and a blessing.

And I didn't mention the main thing: Itai. Every time I'm outside, he's inside, and vice versa. The connection between us is a condition for maintaining this business.

Do the children find themselves involved in your Arugot activities, or do they not care?

It's like their playground. Our house has a garden, which

all the neighborhood kids like to come and take care of. When the subject that we are dealing with in Arugot is interesting, it automatically draws the children to itself. Before each workshop, the children harvest the plants for me, and ask "What are you teaching? What are you doing? What did you do?" And they make bath bombs for their bath, and prepare anti-lice oil for the baby, and when she wakes up at night they tell me: "Put lavender on her," because these are the concepts they hear; these are the raw materials of our lives.

When I'm out of the house a lot, it's hard on them. When there are intense periods, like now, for example, when there are many workshops and lectures, they are like, what is it called in music? Oh, a metronome. They are like a metronome that tells you if you're on target. They are my pulse. I know that if red lights start lighting up in the house, then for everyone's benefit I'd better down-gear.

All kinds of investors tried to join us and be part of Arugot, but they said I'd have to be in Tel Aviv three days a week. I told them: "Thanks, but no thanks. We'll stay here, everything's fine, once a week is enough for me." I'm simply in a different space from the one people are used to in Western society.

So your question is very relevant. How does a woman do both? But that's how I feel, in my own case. It's not a man's business; my business is committed to harmony before it's committed to results. That's what I believe.

So you don't have pangs of conscience?

What do you mean? I see that you're not a woman. For mothers, pangs of conscience are built-in, an integral part of motherhood. For mothers, there are always pangs of conscience.

Okay, now I've calmed down; I thought you were Superwoman. But Esther, forgive me, I want to return with you to the past. Tell me again about the economic transition from concocting ointments for neighbors and the establishment of the Arugot brand. I'm being persistent that you talk about this because I'm sure there are men or women who'll read the book and say, "Wow! I also want to move my creation out into the world." For example, let's say that someone makes various Bach flower essences, and she wants to have a brand like Arugot, but the leap is a big one. Help her.

Right. There has been a wild jump in my business in the last four years. In the first two years, I was alone, and then Itai came into the business with me, and at that point, there really was a jump. Under the surface, on the hidden levels, I think the jump began when we merged. I feel that whenever there is a connection between us, when we work on the same frequency and hold a common image in our heads, then there are jumps.

So your advice is to get married, and to have your spouse as a business partner?

I was pregnant with my third son, and I reached a crossroads: either I fearfully keep the project to myself, keeping everything small, because I no longer had my licenses from the Ministry of Health, or I dare to grow. And Itai gave me strength. He said to me: "Look there's a demand for your products. Why are you stuck on the level of twenty neighbors and seventeen friends as customers?"

And then?

And then we made a marketing move for Arugot. It started with writing. I started to write a column in a women's newspaper, and an online blog. I got feedback that people are interested in this, that it's not something that's just my

personal hobby. I would tell about the period in which I lived in the desert, and at the same time, I would publish a recipe for making soap. I think that writing led to the first breakthrough, because readers began to ask and to take an interest. As a result, we built a website, we created a virtual presence, something which is very important these days to actually accomplish things. My writing was a very significant leap which generated invitations to give lectures. The lectures generated a lot of exposure, from universities and colleges too, as well as health conferences. In such conferences, all at once, five hundred people ask for the deodorant you were talking about in a lecture. At this point we decided to buy tools from abroad and set up an industrial production line, we added workers, and the rest is history.

I'm glad for your answer on behalf of all those who will read it.

Why?

Because, in fact, you probably didn't get any money for those articles.

For some of them I did, and for some of them I didn't.

And the lectures, it may also be that you didn't receive any money for some of them.

Right. For some of them I did, and for some of them I didn't.

The lectures and writing were a combination of exposure and contributing.

Right. Completely.

You just contributed. Recipes, advice. No marketing, you contributed. Then people became addicted to your contributions.

True, you remind me now of something important about the blog. The blog was free of course; I started a blog entirely for

myself, as a personal therapy. Suddenly, I saw a day later that two hundred people entered the blog; I didn't understand where they came from. And then the two hundred became five hundred, and then a thousand. Suddenly I saw that the blog was gaining momentum, that I have hundreds of people to write to. At this stage, the dynamics had already begun, since people started asking medical questions: What do you do about worms in the intestines? About insomnia? About eczema in the skin? I started sharing recipes and my personal experience.

Why did I say that your answer pleased me? Because I meet a lot of people who are on the way, who are at the construction stage, and who have a lot to contribute. They tell me "When customers come, I have something to give them," but it doesn't work that way. I tell them "You have something to give? Do so *now*. The income from it will come later."

I totally agree.

Another question, with your permission. You touched on it, but I want to dig a little deeper. In my book, I write that just as one's talents are a clue to their mission, so too, one's failures are a hint at their mission, or they accompany them on their mission; they are necessary. You talked about what happened in childhood, being an outsider, and also about the illness in India, which was a deep trigger for your connection to yourself and re-healing, something really terrific.

Another aspect of the failure: the helplessness. We arrived as a couple who had just married. I came, a shadow of my former self, to the doctor, and he presumed to tell me what my body is capable of? Someone has programmed this body a little before you, dear doctor.

Only later did I realize how shocking it was. As far as

the doctor was concerned, it was "Okay, so you don't have a cycle, so you'll never get pregnant. That's it. Next patient." But that's all? Our abilities are useless here? All options are doomed to failure here?

The failures you're talking about were very significant for me. My Mom says all the time: "I have to send the articles about you in the newspaper to your teachers." I asked her, "What for, Mom? Who remembers them, and why you think that they remember me?"

My mother told me that at every parent-teacher conference, they would tell her and my father, "Listen, this girl, she's not good at anything." Once, at a parent-teacher conference, my father said to the teacher, "Well, we heard all the teachers, now just tell us at least one thing that she's good at. One thing." And the teacher thought for a long time...

I'm in shock.

My mother loves to tell this story, for some reason. Then the teacher said, "She's not good at anything."

This story is insane.

Many times my mother asks me if grade school left me traumatized, but I don't remember anything about it. I just remember that I had a comic notebook, that I drew pictures and wrote stories in. I remember making bracelets at that age from threads, and I would sell them near my grandmother's house in the Old City. I was very attached to her, to my grandmother, may she rest in peace. She was such an authentic Persian lady; she put the whole idea of working with raw materials in my head. She would sew and crochet, and there were only whole spices in her kitchen. Grade school itself, however, is erased from my mind.

But for my parents, it was a traumatic life experience. At

every parent-teacher conference for eight years, my teachers told them I had nothing. Thank God it was before the era that pushes pills at anyone who can't sit.

Is that so? You think that if you were a girl in our generation, they would give you Ritalin?

Definitely. For a while, I was a teacher in a special education school. Breakfast for every child? Ritalin, before anything else. And that's, apropos of the book you're writing, precisely the prime recipe for extinguishing a person's knowledge of what they're good at.

Because what are they telling the children by giving them Ritalin? They're telling them: "You need external help to join the herd, because you can't sit still like everyone else. We'll give you a pill and fix you. You're just a machine, like a car. Go to the garage, the doctor will fix you."

When you ask a six-year-old boy what he likes to do — he knows. He knows from the age of four what he likes to do. I see my daughter; she loves to do certain things on which she will get stuck all day, and another daughter – loves other things. These are indications; what you're good at and what you like to do, and provide clues to what you need to do in life.

As for failure, I don't know whether it's a hint as much as an alarm clock. Failure wakes you up in the area in which you failed. If you recall for a moment the failure you had, the bubble in your imagination bursts, and you land in a reality that will reflect what you really have to do, you understand? You may have imagined that you should, for example, set up a company, but it fails, so your bubble bursts. Ninety percent of the time we are fed, and misled, by the bubble, by our thoughts, by the mistaken plans for the future and by the nonsense of the past.

Failure brings you back to the present, period. No games. You realize what resources you actually do have, and those are what you work with, and thus you progress to the next step.

If we've already talked about talents, let's go back to this matter of the physical world, the material, the earth, the connection to the crudest things, the juiciness of life, the mud – how do you relate to these materials?

I really like physicality and matter. There is a perception, one that seems Christian to me, which says that spirituality is detached from matter, that a spiritual person is detached from matter. In my opinion, spirituality is everywhere, in every grain of earth. When I dive down with the children to plant winter roots, I feel that infinity is there. You're part of the cosmic experience. You're simply being embraced by the experience. It's possible to speak theoretically about spirituality for hours, and about philosophy too. But everything is found in the material world, in physicality.

It's like walking around a spring and imagining what it would be like to swim in it, and then someone comes along and pushes you in – by then, words are irrelevant, right?

The Maggid (Preacher) of Mezritz would say that this is what is written in Psalms, "The earth is full of Your possessions." Wherever I go, I discover that I can possess You. Spirituality is in every flower, every smile, every side street.

That's beautiful.

Say, you said before that when you came to Sde Boker you met "principled, values-based secularism." My question is — do you think that if you had continued on the path of ethical secularism, had married an ethical secularist, and had established a secular Arugot, would it have looked the same? Would it feel the same?

Wow... that's a good question. I need two days to think about it.

I don't think everything would look the same, that's perfectly clear. I could be that I would still say that I was only an emissary, and that I was a pipe, the same sentences I say now, but then I'd say I'm a messenger of the universe (not of God)... Still, I feel that the connection to God simply gives me true humility. That's the difference in my opinion.

In other words, in your assessment, if you were an ethical secularist, then you would say "I accomplished all this *by my own strength and power*"?

I'll tell you the difference. I don't know about "*by my own strength and power*," but if I were not religious, I would take the project more seriously. I would identify much more closely with Arugot. I would say "I *am* Arugot. It's my life's work — it's me." You understand? I'd take Arugot even more seriously than I do now.

In psychology, that's called "attachment."

Look, first of all, my present faith-based thinking makes me connected to life; it's thinking that puts things in proportion. Giving birth also puts things in proportion. And children too. This thinking frees me from the feeling that they and I are one, and that I am identical to them.

There is a central management in the world, and everyone has a different relationship with it. Arugot is an entity and a being in and of itself. During stressful times, I tell Itai that Arugot is like a Tamagotchi app: You constantly have to feed and sustain it. But the company really came into being by itself. I have no idea how buyers came, and how press

reporters came, and people who want to purchase or be part of Arugot came. The process took place by itself, like some jellyfish living in the world. I see a lot of people who set up business and the business became them; it swallowed them up. The business is completely identified with them.

And I know that even if we sell Arugot (God forbid, hopefully we won't be subjected to such temptations), nothing will happen to me, because Arugot isn't me. I have a path in life, which has nothing to do with Arugot. At the moment it's expressed in Arugot, but I am myself, not Arugot. If Arugot didn't exist, we would find another "excuse" to impact others, another means.

Who knows, it could be that you've accompanied Arugot up to this point, and someone else needs to take it from here and make it universal, or something like that. Who knows?

People always tell me, 'Arugot is another child.' But it really isn't another child. Now it's my sweetest and most joyful device, but it's not my child.

We didn't talk about it so much, but I feel that many times, in the context of the word "mission," we use all kinds of explosive terms such as "devotion" and so forth. I feel that if there wasn't something very basic, I call it "a sweetness" in this project, I wouldn't be here even for a day and a half. In two days I would already have closed down the business. I don't because it's simply fun for me.

On the one hand, I don't agree with you, because it's *you* who makes it fun. On the other hand, I agree with you that there is no obligation to suffer; destiny isn't suffering.

Beyond what we said about giving: Let's say someone is reading the book now and dreams of actualizing her creation, her mission in the world. What can you tell her? How can you help her?

I think that starting small is the best advice. There is a lot of confusion today that "success = go for big," and because of Facebook, all of you is exposed to the outside world, and anyone can see what condition you're in, so you have to prove yourself. We have a lost a bit of the blessing that is in the unseen, the concealed. We forget that sometimes people, especially women, want their own private place to be blessed in. And while it may be that for men success equals brand, name, fame, something big, empire, as we talked about, I feel that many times women achieve inner gratification from something small. My advice is to take the first small steps.

It's unbelievable how many imaginary barriers women have in their heads today. I am accompanying someone who makes a line of clothes. She's sewing at home right now, but already she asks herself "what will happen if I go public when there is a demand for two hundred items?" and she doesn't want to hire a seamstress, so she's afraid to go forward. She's already thinking ten steps ahead, and because of that, she's not taking the first one. Many times, when you take the first step, reality shows you an escalator going in another direction, which you didn't plan on, and you take that.

I started with crafts, not plants. I worked at "Reshimo," a cultural center in the Nachlaot neighborhood in Jerusalem. We set up ancient crafts space, something like a tent, and taught women the craft of basket-weaving. But at some point, I realized that the basket-weaving craft is detached from me, and that I can't express myself through wool-dying art. Suddenly, the plants I learned about at Reidman College, in the most boring course as far as I was concerned "kidnapped" me. I have no other definition.

I feel that we, as human beings, are very fond of well-defined paths, and of knowing where we are going, but we aren't ready to take the first step faithfully, in the simplest way. Many times, if you take just the first step, which can even be just opening a Facebook page, or advertising among your neighbors that you sell Judaica, or knitted *kippot*, after you take that first step, suddenly someone says that right now they have a family event and they need twenty units. Take the first step, "Make a needle's eye-sized opening for Me, and I will make a building-sized opening for you."

Yes, it sounds like a cliché, but for some reason, the barrier is like a screen in the brain. There are a lot of obstructions in the way of the first step, and I have a lot of friends who want to open something, such as a therapeutic center, or classes for women, but the "nay-sayers" overpower them, and nothing is done in reality, in practice.

Shut the brain. Shut your mind, get rid of fantasies. What do you need? You need a room? Come on, ok, we rented a room. How many people do you need? Fifteen? Ok, we got fifteen together. Start. There is no company yet, there is no name yet, but take the first step, start.

I tell you, I feel that everyone is captive to being normal, "square."

People take "normalcy" to the wrong place, in my opinion. The Sages write in the Passover Haggadah about the wicked son: "By excluding himself from the norm, he became heretical" but their intent isn't "be like everyone else and lose your unique shade." They mean that when you disconnect yourself from caring about the community, from concern for the community — then you're a heretic; it's not about not being "normal". You won't find the concept of "normal" in Judaism. You'll find "holy," you'll find "pure," but you won't find "normal." The story here is being "normal." In my opinion, it's like missing the essential point itself, like bypassing the main point. The point is, you have to be really attached to the community.

I think as you do — but just the opposite. When you connect to *yourself*, automatically your spring will affect the outside world, the community. Understand? I could tell myself a story that I was meant to be a teacher of special education and this will be my contribution. I do understand children very well, in fact, but I think I might have had a very unhappy life in that profession, if I had believed this story. This is a very strong barrier, especially for the religious public. It's very nice to be a teacher and give of yourself, or be in the social work profession, and it's clear if you are, you're contributing to the common good, and are a "woman of valor" and so on. It's very hard to say no to these professions.

But if the woman I was talking about really connects to herself, then she'll discover that what really interests her now is to produce clothes, and fashion attracts and excites her. Very materialistic and superficial, isn't it, being fascinated by dress patterns? It's even a little egotistical on her part, isn't it?

I say: No! Through fashion, you affect the world, and make a difference.

Thank you, Esther. I could sit with you for hours, and enjoy both your silence and all the truths that come forth from your mouth, but the truth is that I already got a lot of this interview, more than I could have expected, and I hope that the men and the women who read what you had to say will too. Thank you for all your insights. May you be blessed with all the blessings, and may your light shine far and wide.

THE STORY OF A MESSENGER

FROM EGOISM TO ALTRUISM

I first met Oded in my car. More precisely, I met his voice there. It's a quiet, calm and soothing voice. He was giving the type of lecture that makes you meditate, burned on a CD that a friend gave me with a smile spread on his face.

Then I met him face-to-face, and I encountered depth and sweetness. His look gave the impression that he was someone both hovering in the upper worlds, and at the same time had both feet planted on the ground.

Oded, 43, is a popular lecturer in Hassidism, and he also teaches Tai Chi and meditation in colleges and private settings; he's married, has five children, and lives on a cooperative settlement. Simply put, he transfers the money he earns to a common communal fund, and he draws money from the fund according to the needs of his family.

Reminds you of the kibbutz of yesteryear? You're not mistaken, but it's not exactly a kibbutz.

I am interested in knowing how and why in a capitalistic world, one chooses to live in a way so contrary to human nature.

I wonder how to make a connection between Tai Chi and Jewish life.

I am interested in the connection that many people, not only Oded, make between Eastern spirituality and Judaism.

A large table, Rabbi Baruch Shalom Ashlag once said, is a table with a large distance between its extremes. And a great man? The same. Oded has quite a few extremes. I know from experience — this promises to be an interesting life story.

So I asked him to start from the beginning.

I was born in Jerusalem, and I lived there until I was twenty-seven. My father is from Europe; my mother's family has been in Israel for fourteen generations. My father and mother were born into "pure" secular homes. It's impossible to say that they had either fondness for or resentment toward religiously observant people, because such people didn't interest them, and indeed the Jewish religion didn't interest them, they didn't even recite *Kiddush* (the blessing over wine) on Friday night.

When I reached bar-mitzvah age, thirteen, my father asked me if I wanted to go on a trip abroad, or do I prefer, like most children in the class, to be called up to the Torah in the synagogue, a traditional Jewish custom. I answered that I wanted both... He agreed, and I was called up to the Torah.

I was later accepted to the Hebrew University High School. That's what it was called: "the University High School." It was considered prestigious and elitist — suitable for someone who is interested in the exact sciences. I was always drawn to the scientific fields, to physics and mathematics. I have no idea how that relates to what I do today.

When I was fifteen years and two months old, I met my wife. Do you get it? My wife, Yiska, is my first and only woman on earth.

After high school I enlisted in the army, enthusiastic and

excited about the idea of serving in the army, in the infantry, being out in the field as much as possible, and I found myself, like all my friends from high school, in the Nahal Brigade.

The problem was that after two months, I wanted to leave. I felt that military service was really not what I thought it would be. They tried to assign me to be the liaison officer of the deputy battalion commander, perhaps there I would find myself, but I suffered greatly. I hated the army, I really hated it.

So far I had lived a straightforward, typical life. If you have to go to school — you go to school, if you have to go to the army – you go to the army. I did everything with the guys: we went to the Scouts, we went into the IDF, and after being discharged from the army, at the age of twenty-two, I made my first trip abroad. *Our* first trip – Yiska went with me.

Our first trip was for a year. It was a trip to India, Thailand, Nepal, Vietnam, and Tibet. We weren't exposed to any spiritual content there, except for a little silence workshop for ten days, where I first encountered Vipassana meditation. Don't tell anyone, but I wasn't completely silent; I fudged, cut corners. I wasn't really serious about it.

Then we returned to Israel and got married. After the wedding, I started trying to figure out "what I want to do when I grow up," so I studied carpentry for a year. I even have a carpentry certificate.

After a year of studying carpentry, I saw that it wasn't for me, I was too bored, and so I went to study theater at the Nissan Nativ Acting Studio for one year. There, too, I realized that studying theater isn't for me, so I transferred to studying cinema.

I studied at the Sam Spiegel Film & Television School in Jerusalem for a year, and I ran away from there too...

Why?

I felt that I was deceiving myself, my soul. I felt that they weren't teaching me to make beautiful and professional films, but rather they were teaching me how to create a fiction, how to patch patches together so that they look real. It made me think there was nothing real about cinema.

I remember that they asked us to make a documentary, to find an interesting figure and make a movie about them, so I made a film about myself.

As the expression goes, "I only know how to tell about myself..."

Exactly so. Learning cinema was so external to me. It's true, they loved me there, and asked me to stay on, but I left.

I don't understand how someone who presumes to be a student of the exact sciences goes to study film and theater. What's the connection?

I studied those things because there's something else that turned me on a lot, other than physics. I wanted to be famous. I thought that through acting one could become famous faster than through physics. How many famous physicists do you know?

And what's the connection between being famous and Tai Chi? How did you get to that?

All in all, after I left cinema studies, I went on living, without studying or working. I had all the time in the world to do what I wanted, but at the same time, there was also a strong feeling of disappointment and being unfulfilled.

How so?

I didn't understand what was bothering me. We had no lack of money, and I married a woman I love. I said to myself,

what are you missing, man? All in all, I was happy, I wasn't depressed, God forbid, but I was happy, however there was an unresolved issue that poked me deep inside.

At that time, a friend of Yiska, my wife, suggested that she join a Tai Chi class in Jerusalem. She described Tai Chi as "enjoyable exercise." My wife tried it, and after a few lessons felt a connection and suggested that I join too. I refused, of course; what would I do in a girls' gymnastics class?

Actually, Tai Chi is obviously not merely exercise, but a combination of calisthenics and breathing. Originally, this was a martial art doctrine, but it's slow and focused, not like karate. And it's definitely not only for girls.

After two months, Yiska was more assertive and just enrolled me in a beginner's course on her own. They told me that I was already registered, so I might as well go. So I went.

And what? Did you connect right away?

Listen, Moshe, when I left, I felt high. I felt that finally, something managed to create a connection point in me, a point of quiet and contemplation I never experienced before. This fascinated me. An hour and a half of silence: make a movement with your body, stop, now breathe, reflect. It made me say "wow, what an island of sanity." Only then I realized how noisy my soul was.

Tai Chi grabbed us powerfully, both me and my wife. We had plenty of time, because we hardly worked, and even when we did, it was at something temporary and part-time, so we found ourselves practicing Tai Chi by ourselves at home, every day.

Then the subject of meditation came to Israel. After Tai Chi and relaxation, we would sit quietly, contemplating, concentrating on one point. Both of us had already decided in our hearts that this was our direction, so we wanted to find out where Tai Chi was practiced most seriously. We were told that there's an area in China called "Shanxi" and that's where the foundation of Tai Chi is.

We checked details, place, costs, and we went there, without too many questions or misgivings. We didn't go as tourists, like on the first trip. We went to study and to practice Tai Chi.

So just like that, in the middle of life, a married couple, instead of having children — go to China?

Yes. And not for a month or two. For two years.

Two years?

We stayed in the Shanxi region of the Far East for eight months. At first, we studied, and then we took a teaching course, and then they appointed us to be team leaders, because they saw that we were serious and dedicated.

At one point, we felt that we had exhausted the subject, and we just wanted to tour the area. We decided that we would leave where we had been staying, in order to travel to all sorts of places in the Far East for "silence tours"; we would rent a house and not talk for two weeks. We would come to an advance agreement with the landlords that we wouldn't talk, and asked them in advance to bring us breakfast, lunch, water bottles, and we'll pay them as much as necessary. Of course, our landlords were delighted with this arrangement.

So there the two of us were in one room, silent, not talking, not uttering a word. What did we do? We contemplated, and we went hiking through villages, forests, mountainous landscapes, all without conversing at all, for whole weeks at a time. We would sit down to eat and not utter a single word.

I've never heard of anyone doing such a thing.

Today it seems incredible to me, and a bit nuts, but at that time we used silence as a kind of medicine. We got to know ourselves, but not only that; in fact, our contact with God came from this. I don't mean the God of the Jews who revealed Himself on Mount Sinai and gave the Torah to the people of Israel, but something more abstract.

God? In China?

Yes. In this silence, you discover that there is something besides you, and it's alive, it lives within you, and you have a connection with it. And you also find that when you have a relationship with it, you feel that you're living as you should, and when you have no such relationship, you feel disconnected.

And all this time the two of you, both you and Yiska, remained silent?

Yes, for hours and hours. Our schedule was get up at six in the morning, have an hour of contemplation, and then practice Tai Chi for three hours or four hours, then we would have lunch, eating coconut, and go to sleep for two hours. At four o'clock we did more Tai Chi practice, at six o'clock we practiced contemplation for an hour, then we had a Dim Sum dinner or something like that, and then we retired to our bedroom and went to sleep.

This went on for a long time, almost a year. We would zero in on one village, then a month later we would decide to move to another village, but we would do exactly the same thing everywhere.

And what was happening in Israel all this time? Two years is a long time.

Yeah, right. While we were in China, they discovered

cancer in a very close childhood friend of mine. He got sick at the age of twenty, and then he recovered, but while we were on our tours, they found more signs of the disease. We corresponded, and he told me about his struggles. His illness seemed terminal, but then he recovered again, miraculously. It looks like his closeness to death shocked him, and he became religious and got engaged. I was invited to the wedding.

Silences are important, but you don't miss your best friend's wedding, right? There's a limit.

That's obviously true, but two days after the wedding, we were back in the East, this time in India. And my friend, the new husband, had already become a consummate strictly religious guy, and provided us with religious books and CDs before we returned to the East.

About what?

The writings of Rav Kook, Rabbi Nachman, Rav Ashlag, all sorts of stuff, and CDs with lectures by various lecturers.

And did you connect?

Yes. We loved the aspect of Judaism which was presented there — less obsessive, a kind of light *Hassidism*. The material sounded spiritual to us, and it suited what we were doing at that time. It didn't bother us that it was religious, and the material began to seep into our activities.

On Yom Kippur, for example, we decided to fast in silence. I remember that we also had a day of asking for forgiveness. We sat for a whole day thinking about whom we should apologize to, and whom we have to forgive; for example, apologize to Mother and apologize to Father. Each of us did this separately, but we planned it together. It was very special.

And weren't there differences of opinion about this between

you, or about other things? It sounds like the two of you wanted Judaism equally. I don't know such couples.

You're right. There were disagreements too. After a year and ten months, my wife felt that she wanted to go home. We both felt, even before discussing it, that Israel was our home. Afterward, we talked quite a bit, between silences, about whether to return to Israel or to stay in India.

It was clearer to her that Israel was our home than it was to me. I thought that maybe we should go back to China, or even better — that we should stay in India, where you can live your whole life without working. With the little bit of money our parents were able to give to us, a fraction of what you spend on mortgage payments in Israel, it's possible to buy a house in India and not work even one day for the rest of your life; you can just sit around and do what you'd like to.

But my wife saw it differently: "I want children" she said. "Children should be raised in Israel, not here." I agreed with her, and we didn't argue about it, but we hesitated a lot because I, with my realistic mind, still made financial calculations: I said to Yiska: "Maybe we should stay here in India nonetheless? What's so bad about not working? What's so bad about where we are? We have a house on the beach; if we want, we can run Tai Chi workshops now and then, and so we can even make some money. In Israel, we'll have to work most of the time just in order to survive, to get by. When will we practice Tai Chi if we return to Israel? When will we meditate?"

But you don't say "no" to a woman.

Right. We returned to Israel, not to Jerusalem but to the Jerusalem corridor, to the Aminadav moshav, to raise a family and raise the children in the atmosphere of the Land

of Israel. At Aminadav, we established a Tai Chi center and started to run workshops, and we made a living from that for a good few years. We had children, and at the same time, I taught in all kinds of places. I taught special populations too: battered women, children in distress, and others. I taught them to look at themselves and at their thoughts; I taught them how to move aside when anger or fear comes. I practiced Tai Chi with them, so that they could connect to themselves. The One above sent me all sorts of people to help.

A short time after we returned to Israel, my friend who had become religious died. A few weeks after his wedding, the disease attacked him again; this time it was fast, and he ascended to heaven at the age of age twenty-seven. But sometimes, when someone is a messenger for you, his mission continues even after his death. His wife, his widow, succeeded in recovering from the trauma over the course of time, and she remarried. At that time, she worked as a secretary in Jerusalem, at a yeshiva called "Machon Meir," and there she met Rabbi Reuven Fierman. We didn't know about any of this, of course. She must have thought we would like his lectures, and so she taped four cassettes, put them in an envelope, and sent it to us without saying whom it was from. My wife and I listened to the tapes and said: "Wow, what's this beautiful thing?" We were blown away.

The telephone number of the yeshiva was on the tape, so we called them and bought more tapes. We swallowed those up too. After a few months, I called again and asked if I could meet this fascinating lecturer. They said, "Sure, where are you from?" I answered that I live near Jerusalem. "Well, Rabbi Fierman teaches in Jerusalem" they answered me. I couldn't believe my ears; Rabbi Fierman lectures once a week fifteen minutes from my home?

I arrived, all excited, in the year 2002, at a class on a Wednesday morning, together with the yeshiva students. But when I saw him, I was really turned off. He had a long beard and a black hat. When I had heard his lectures, I had imagined someone entirely different. My parents had no problem with religious people, but nevertheless, I grew up in Jerusalem; there's almost no chance that a secular boy in Jerusalem will have no serious antagonism towards the strictly religious. Jerusalem is a city of struggles.

When I saw him, I thought that now was the time to run away; to be a spiritual person, you don't need this disguise, a long beard, and a big black hat.

But I couldn't just walk away. I was addicted to the depths of thought I had heard from him. I loved every word that came out of his mouth. It was a critical moment, "to be or not to be," and I chose "to be." I said to myself "If this is the same person who speaks on the tapes, then let him wear whatever he wants, I don't care; the main thing is to keep hearing what he has to say."

Indeed, your fears came true; you became religious. You had a chance to escape, and you knowingly went in.

Yes. Slowly, or quickly, depending on whom you ask, my wife and I started to observe more and more of Jewish law. I began to pray and to study Torah, Gemara, Hassidism, and Kabbalah.

Previously, when we would go on errands, especially in Beit Shemesh, which then wasn't as ultra-Orthodox as it is today, I remember telling my wife, "Do you know what I like about this area? You don't see religious people all the time,

it's not like Jerusalem." Now she teases me about it...

And you found that there's something in Judaism that's not in Far Eastern spirituality?

I think that after all the years of spiritual search, both of us saw Judaism as something deeper and more fundamental than Eastern spirituality, and also as something that better meets our needs. We encountered a spiritual, structured and orderly way of life that goes down into detail, into the person's life, one that doesn't leave room for doubt and uncertainty, one that takes people by the hand in a perfectly disciplined way; it provides discipline within family life, within community life, within society, within marriage.

You're describing a return to religious practice that went very quickly, particularly for people who had lived such a slow-paced life. How do you explain the quick pace?

It seems to me that our long retreats and contemplations had prepared us for this.

And here too, you and your wife were on the same page, and moving at the same pace. That's amazing.

At first, when I decided I to wear a *kippa*, a skullcap, as religious men do, I remember my wife saying, "Listen, it's too soon." Indeed, people would ask me, "What, you're becoming religious?" and I had no answer for them. So I said to her, "Okay, I'll take off the *kippa*." I took the *kippa* off, and I started to cry, so she said to me, "Ok, then, wear a *kippa*, we'll manage somehow."

And yet, why did you go "all the way" with Judaism, and not with Eastern spirituality?

According to most Eastern teachings, if you want to be serious, you have to isolate yourself, to be a monk or a Buddhist, without a wife, without a family and children,

without work, and thus there was no option, as far as we were concerned, to "go all the way," because we were already married, and we didn't want to break up.

In fact, there was a moment, while we were in the East, when I presented my wife with the option of going to isolate ourselves in some cave in Tibet or in northern India, each of us separately, for a year or a year and a half, but I saw that she turned pale at the very thought. I thought of this idea because I wanted to reach the apex of Eastern spirituality, and being at the top and most serious in Eastern terms means going to caves alone. Luckily, she didn't agree.

I think that we once got a hint to return to Israel along the way, while we were still in India. In the mornings, after an hour of contemplation, each of us, separately, used to take a book that they liked, a book with a spiritual message, open it at random, and see what message they would get for that day. In fact, today I understand that this is problematic in the opinion of the Jewish Sages, but then that's what we used to do. My wife would do it with a Book of Psalms.

Psalms? Where did you get a Book of Psalms? From the newly-religious friend?

No. From a different friend. A secular guy who lives in Jerusalem heard that we were in the Far East for almost two years, and he began to worry about us, cut off from everything Jewish, so he decided to send us a full Bible that he got in the army, and then other Jewish texts. It's funny, because he's not really religious, but he had a part in our return to Jewish practice.

I had all kinds of spiritual books that I would open, and one day, after we finished our contemplation, when my wife who had already finished and went for a walk, I reached for a certain book, but the Psalms lay over it. I went with the flow; I said to myself "What difference does it make what book I take? Ok, today I'll take the Psalms, what do I care?" I opened the Book of Psalms, in a random place, and looked inside. A page with a lot of psalms was there, and my finger was on Psalm 127. I began to read:

Shir ha-Ma'alot (a Song of ascents to the Holy Temple)

For Shlomo (King Solomon):
If the Lord does not build a house, its builders will work at it in vain;
If the Lord does not guard a city, its guards' efforts are futile.
It is of no use for you to rise early and stay up late,
You who eat the bread of toil;
He gives His beloved sleep.
Lo, the inheritance of the Lord is sons: the fruit of the womb is a reward.
As arrows in the hand of a mighty man, so are the children of one's youth.
Blessed is the man who has filled up his quiver with them:
They will not be put to shame when they speak with their enemies at the gate.

This psalm surprised me. "How can this be?" I said to myself. "I was just talking to Yiska about establishing a home, a family, and children!"

But wait, at that point we didn't have enough money to return to Israel; we had been wandering around for two years in a world without work. We thought we would go to work before we returned to Israel, maybe in Europe. We started to make inquiries; we asked Europeans where we can work there, so that we could return to Israel with a little money to raise a family. But on the other hand, we didn't really want to travel to Europe to work, after two years of Tai Chi and silence, we didn't really want to make such a sharp turn and return to civilization.

Could *Tehillim* (Psalms) have given us a message? *The inheritance of the Lord is sons: the fruit of the womb is a reward.* I told myself "Only a day and a half ago I spoke about this with my wife, and the answer is right here: "God will send you money. Do you want to start a family? Go do it...."

That day, my wife kept saying she had something to tell me. "Every day I open *Tehillim*, and this morning I opened to a Psalm which spoke about exactly what we spoke about two days ago." We opened the book and discovered that we had read the same Psalm! We didn't know what to do with this revelation, and we spun around like two crazy people. We didn't know whom to speak to, who would understand our excitement over the message, and then we decided to go and consult an Indian guru we had met on our first journey, whom we greatly admired. We told him the whole story. He looked at us, and then answered in his broken English, but with a lot of wisdom (he understood what we hadn't yet understood):

"The world has spoken. Go to Israel and have children. Everything will be okay."

Thank God, we returned to Israel, and afterward I began to study Torah regularly in the mornings in Jerusalem, and in the evenings I still went to teach Tai Chi.

And how did it work out, Tai Chi combined with the Judaism? Why did you decide to connect them?

I didn't decide on my own, I went to ask a rabbi. I told him I had been teaching Tai Chi already many years, and it started in China. I asked him if I needed to change jobs, to stop teaching Tai Chi. He replied no. I tried to challenge his answer, and suggested that perhaps Tai Chi was connected to "idolatry." The rabbi asked "What do you do in Tai Chi? Calisthenics? Breathing?" I told him "yes, that's it." He replied that calisthenics and breathing aren't idolatry. And then he said to me "Whom do you want to teach Tai Chi to the Jewish people? Those who don't know what is idolatry and what's not idolatry? It's *you* who needs to teach it."

So the rabbi gave his blessing to teach Tai Chi, but how did you begin to teach Hassidut?

It happened by itself. At first in small groups, and slowly it grew.

Today Oded teaches at the seminars of the "*Arachim*" ("Values") and "*Nefesh Yehudi*" ("Jewish Soul") organizations, and gives Torah classes to various groups throughout the country.

Why don't you in fact take Tai Chi "all the way?" Why are you spending your time teaching others *Hassidut* instead of just focusing on Tai Chi? Isn't that really your mission? Why don't you open Tai Chi centers all over the country? Why don't you invest most of your time in Tai Chi?

Because my heart is no longer there.

What do you mean? Look, you yourself developed personally through Tai Chi and meditation, and you chose to pass on the knowledge and practice to others before you became religious, and you sensed that you were a faithful messenger for them, and also now you teach Tai Chi in a kosher way — how could your heart no longer be there? Isn't that your mission?

Good question. If had you asked me then, in the past,

"What's the biggest, greatest, most valuable gift you can give to someone else?" I would answer — Tai Chi. But as soon as I entered into the world of the insights and depths of the Torah, my answer has changed. The most I can give a person today is insights from the Torah. It's a much deeper and more comprehensive worldview and life view. If I could teach students Tai Chi and while doing so teach them Torah, everything would be perfect, but that's unprofessional. If you train men and women to teach Tai Chi, you're committed to Tai Chi. That's your profession, that's what you do, and you're also identified with the profession you're connected to. For me, that started to create a conflict, because it was no longer the most valuable thing that I can give you.

Okay, I got an answer. And there is something else you do, silence workshops, right?

Yes. Worldwide it's called "Vipassana," but we jokingly call it "Klipassana," a combination *klipa* (peel) and Vipassana. The idea is that silence can help us strip the outer peels from ourselves. Several times a year, I guide a seminar that changes people's lives.

Klipasana is a slightly different story than Vipassana. I started with the same motive: to give people an opportunity to attend a silence workshop based on holiness. Indeed, in most of the Far East they separate men and women in these workshops, which is beautiful, but in courses in the East, you mustn't do anything religious in the course of the workshop. It's forbidden even to put on *tefillin*, which is a Jewish obligation for men, since among their regulations is a prohibition to engage in any other religious ceremony during these ten days. And the spiritual contents of Vipassana are, of course, Buddhist. In Eastern Vipassana courses, at night, a monk teaches you lessons in Buddhist philosophy.

Today, I'm crushed about Jews practicing Vipassana and nothing else; my heart aches inside me. I shout, I call out and say, "Dear friends, Vipassana is nice, it's good, but it's the tip of the iceberg. Judaism offers so much more."

It's like someone who ate an apple peel, and for him, the peel is the most wonderful, amazing food in the world. But what can you do, there's an apple under the peel! It's true that if someone didn't have *anything* and ate a peel, as far as they are concerned, they discovered a whole world; but we know there's a whole apple there, in comparison with which the peel is indeed tasty, but still, it's just a peel...

Just a minute, I don't understand: From your point of view, a billion Chinese who can connect to Vipassana are wrong?

No, I didn't say they're wrong. I meant to say that if you're Jewish, no different spirituality can fulfill you. For us, other doctrines are deficient. For the Chinese, the Indians, or the Americans — healing, yoga, Buddhism, or Tai Chi, each of these can be a whole and fulfilling theory of life. For the Jew — not.

The Sages said it simply: "The nations of the world have wisdom? Believe it. The nations of the world have Torah? Don't believe it." The whole idea is that we don't believe that their theory of life is more correct and better for us, the Jews, than the Torah we received on Mount Sinai.

As far as wisdom, medicine, sports, music, art, etc., go, there is no problem to learn from the nations of the world. There's much to learn from them.

If so, these Klipassana workshops create an opportunity for you, because you're teaching content that you believe in?

Yes. I no longer engage in silences as I used to, because

this framework isn't a classic "Torah way" and it isn't my way of life now, but the main reason that I continue to do these workshops is the reactions of the participants. Their responses don't let me give up the workshops. These workshops have been running for ten consecutive years, and they have real power.

On the first day of the workshop, some people say, "Are you serious about asking me to sit down now and close my eyes for a few hours? I'm not there. It's not natural for me now." But very quickly I myself feel the power of the workshop, and the responses I get are so strong, so positive, that people come back year after year. We have people who are coming for their fourth time, their fifth time.

There's something else I wanted to talk to you about. You and your family live in a cooperative community; the members even consolidate salaries; this is completely the opposite of the capitalistic reality that we all live in, something reminiscent of the kibbutz of yesteryear.

Indeed, I have been there ten years. It's amazing, and a huge challenge. I am very individualistic; and it's not only me, most of the people who live in our cooperative community are individualists. For all of us, at one stage or another of our lives, it was important to look at reality with a critical, individualistic eye. And yet, we all decided to go against all the mantras we were taught to recite. We take each individual and subjugate them to the will of the group; we take an ordinary person and tell them that they no longer have any money or private property of their own.

To me, that sounds really hard.

On the one hand, that's so, but on the other hand, I think that this kind of communal life has raised me to a higher level.

I'll give you an example of how it works: One day, I gave a lesson in Kiryat Gat and got $300 for it; I went back to the cooperative and immediately went to the treasurer and gave him the whole sum. He was happy, and said that he was waiting for this money; he opened his notebook and recorded the sum of the deposit, as he did every time money is deposited or withdrawn from the cooperative coffers. Now, in principle, everyone has a budget, but sometimes you need some more, so you ask the treasurer for it; this applies particularly those who go to work outside the commune. So I innocently asked the treasurer for $30, because I needed it. He looked at me and shook his head: "I don't have that $300 you just gave me, someone else asked for them already; even if you had brought me an additional $300, I still wouldn't have given you the $30 you asked for..."

You understand, Moshe, what something like that — I gave the treasurer $300 I had just earned, and he wouldn't give me $30 of it — builds inside someone? It wasn't simple. My head and my heart wanted to explode. But that's how the system works.

Wow, that's very powerful. And what's the difference between this and the collective, kibbutz idea at the beginning of its path? It sounds the same to me.

You're right, basically, the concepts are very similar, but there's a difference, at least according to our view. The kibbutzim functioned wonderfully as long as the founders believed in the justice of the idea, of the path, as long as they believed that to live by the principle "everyone gives according to their ability, and receives according to their needs" is the proper path in life. The minute this ideal became eroded, the whole kibbutz concept eroded.

If so, why would you succeed where others failed? What will cause you not to be ideologically and physically eroded?

I will answer you simply. The communal idea can't last when the motive is only social, when I see only my neighbor before me. Why? Because then I start to ask myself "Why should my neighbor, who puts in less than me, take out more than I do?" For this ideal to last in the long run, a divine idea must be involved: you have to see God at every moment. If you live within this triangle — it provides you with infinite power to live an ideal life. That's how I see things now.

What do you mean by the word "triangle"?

Myself, the other person, and God.

If there's only "me and God," that's worthless, because then how would this be expressed in the world? What's the bright idea, to be a hermit in the mountains? The true challenge is to go down to the village and be able to include a wife, children, and work, in your life.

If there is only "me and the other," that won't last either. You need a third Partner Who will give meaning to the connection between us, so that when you and I live together, we see that Partner before our eyes. Our Sages wrote about this in the context of a husband and wife, who must bring the "third Partner" into their lives.

If there are only "God and the other person" without "me" — that's dangerous. Such a person has lost themselves, most likely, and thinks that they are purely spiritual. People like that scare me.

You know, you're amazing. You summed up in a few sentences the central argument of this book: that a human being is special and must give of themselves; that being learned or keeping the *mitzvot* (commandments) without giving to others is incomplete; and that the messenger is more focused and dedicated when they are connected to the Higher Power. It's fascinating, this idea of a triangle.

Thanks.

And as far as you're concerned, if I understand correctly, your monetary way of life, which you believe we all should live by, is also part of your mission, right?

The answer is, yes, even though I understand that it's very complicated, and something really tremendous must happen before people will understand and sense that greedy, piggish capitalism isn't our direction as a people, and as a country. I believe that that's what Israeli society will look like in the future, not what it looks like today.

Amen. Now I'll change subject with your permission: The *Admor* (Grand Rabbi) of Slonim writes, and I present this approach in detail in the book, that our mission is also related to the failures we experienced: the failure being either a time when some strong desire overcame us, or a significant event we once experienced, or a crisis, or a personality trait that we can't fix like anger, control, pride, jealousy, or an area in which we find it difficult to succeed. The question is, can you can see in yourself a point of failure, through which you can see how the Higher Source has focused you on the mission you fulfill today?

Yes. I think my failure is publicity lust. As I told you, I wanted to be famous, so I was attracted to theater and film studies. Something in me thought that if everyone would know how talented I am, then finally I'd calm down, since then I'd know I probably really am talented. Only when everyone would say "Wow, he's unique, there's no one like him" would I know that there really is no one like me.

That fault in me, a desire for fame, was one of the reasons why I didn't set up a website, and that's why I asked you to change my name in the book and blur my identity. I know that I could be very famous in my field. How many people do you know combine Tai Chi with Judaism? Combine Vipassana and Judaism? I have unique skills.

Tomorrow, if I wanted to, I could be the famous "Rabbi Oded," and publish books, and be invited to appear abroad. It's not easy for me to deal with this desire, and I can't say that I have overcome it 100 percent. So, on the one hand, my desire for fame is a "failure," but on the other hand, the fact that I'm aware of this desire protects me. Thanks to the fact that now I'm wary of publicity, I check myself all the time anew; I ask myself what genuinely motivates me to make a difference others, what is my real inner motivation, and so I correct myself all the time.

And maybe the fact that you tried to find yourself for a few years and didn't succeed, the restlessness that led you to keep searching, was a failure, isn't that so? It's surely frustrating to study carpentry for a year, theater for a year, film for a year, to dig well after well and not find oil — that's a kind of failure too. But without this restlessness, you wouldn't have gone to your first Tai Chi lesson, even if your wife had already paid for it. The quiet you found in Tai Chi, which swept you away to find your destiny in the world, was the result of an intense internal clamor, from your failure to find peace.

I agree with you. I just remembered that I was taught in China that Tai Chi is like litmus paper for consciousness. Within a few moments of practice, you realize where your mind is located, whether you're focused or not. I agree with you that my lack of focus was kind of failure. I see this lack

of focus today in my students.

In conclusion, I would like to read to you a passage written by Rabbi Kook and ask you what do you think of it, okay? To me, in this passage, Rabbi Kook explains beautifully what you're going through: your desire to withdraw into yourself, to pray and to be by yourself as opposed to going out to fulfill your mission and influence others:

> The man whose soul shines within him, must be alone a lot. The constant presence of other people's company, people who are usually spiritually obtuse, dims the clear light of his upper soul, and thus his crucial activity diminishes, and instead of the benefit that he could have brought to society by his isolation from it most of the time (since even then the spiritual relationship does not stop, and he faces the entire generation, prays, and conceives of their prominence, the treasure of goodness within them) rather he causes them to decline by virtue of his own decline, because of the darkness that obscures his spirituality by their disquieting company.

> It is very difficult to tolerate society, to meet with people who find themselves, by their very essence, in a completely different world, a world that the personality immersed in noble spiritual processes, who has great moral aspirations, has no contact with. Nevertheless, this discomfort perfects the person and elevates him. The spiritual influence of the exceptional person on the environment, which comes precisely from frequent contact, purifies the environment, and brings a charm of holiness and freedom to everyone with whom he has contact. And this nobility of grace reflects afterward, more

steadily and actively, upon the influencer himself, and he becomes sociable, full of nobility and holiness, which is more elevated than the sacred content that stands in its solitude.

(Rav Kook, "Orot Hakodesh" ("Lights of Holiness"), 3;271).

So where does this passage meet you (as the psychologists say)?

Right on target. He writes beautifully about a difficult feeling that I encounter quite a bit in life. Rabbi Yehuda Ashlag deals extensively with what he calls "the desire to receive for oneself" and "the desire to influence others." These two forces are present in every person. On the one hand, the need to go out is clear to me, and so I go out to teach almost every day, on the other hand, I am attracted to Torah study and prayer; I wish I could pray all day long.

What will happen if you learn less and take care of people more? They need you, don't they?

You're right, but there is a difficult feeling that accompanies me during Torah study: I feel ashamed.

Ashamed of what?

Knowing that I don't know, that my knowledge of Torah is so deficient.

A friend recently asked me why I "got into" Torah study so strongly. I replied that at a certain stage, I realized that if I didn't start studying Torah for a few hours a day, I will die an ignoramus, and this thought shocked me. The point is that the more I study, the more I feel like an ignoramus. I meet people that everyone can see are Torah personalities, all their body cries out Torah, and on the other hand I look at myself and I see how God loves me and open "gates" of the righteous for me, even though I myself am not righteous,

and indeed I'm very far from being so. He loves me, I don't know why. In the phrase of a great Hebrew poet, "I was granted the Light gratis." I should take advantage of it.

So now do you understand why I go out sparingly and avoid publicity? Because I know that I am a zero, and I can't say to myself "I'll go and make an impact, it's okay, I'm good enough." There's no "good enough," I don't even know how to learn properly yet, I'm short so many hours of Gemara learning, I'm not there yet… and it takes a lot of hours a day.

Precisely on this point you and I disagree, Oded, because I say "Pray half an hour less, learn an hour less, and in the hour and a half that you free up, hold another Torah workshop for the public that needs it so much." Although indeed when I look at you I envy your devotion to Torah and prayer.

I don't know, maybe there's something I need to learn from you, and vice versa…

And yet — what bothers you more, your embarrassment at the Torah you don't know, or that don't get out enough to the Jewish people?

It indeed hurts me that people of are disconnected from themselves, from the truth, from God.

Well, that's just it; you should get out and walk around and connect the disconnected. You have the ability, the sensitivity, needed, and have the background, since you connected yourself to yourself. Help them, teach them to connect.

I don't think I'm doing anything myself in my life. Everything is done by He Who's there upstairs, not me.

Sure you're doing things. Who gets up in the morning for prayer and work? God?

I do act somehow, but I have an internal obligation to do everything I do, I can't do otherwise, for prayer, for Torah;

that time is inviolate, I can't cut it down. You think that *in addition* I should go out and teach more every night? That's a tremendous effort, because I would come back very late and I get up early to learn. Mine is an intensive life, extreme, it's a crazy life, and sometimes I look at my life and say to myself, "What is this madness?"

So continuing to teach is just not you?

No, it's not me. I'm convinced of that.

I thank Oded and pack up, amazed at the man, and think:

a. That I could argue with him for days just about his last sentence.

b. That Oded's transition from a life of extreme isolation to communal life, just as his transition from secularism to religiosity, isn't typical of most of the stories of mission. You don't have to experience extremes to find your destiny in the world.

c. That Oded's search is as complex as that of most people. Like many good people, he had to go through many stages on the way to finding his mission, and that this, too, is probably not his last discovery. There are almost certainly some more details in the script that he hasn't yet discovered.

d. How greatly contact with the Higher Power is significant to the focus of your mission.

e. That without a doubt, the world can't exist without Oded, Esther, and Simona.

f. Or without you.

A WORD TO TEACHERS, PARENTS, AND EDUCATORS

What is education? What is its function? Does education mean imparting values? Providing a personal example? Providing tools for life? Setting limits? What is my role as a parent/teacher/educator?

Look at how Rabbi Zvi Yehuda Kook answers the question:

The education of the private individual is moving, from the potential to the actual, from the unknown to the revealed, the power and the talent which are found in the child's soul by nature, or which are by nature it is worthiest of accepting from the various educational influences. *When the educational factors — parents and teachers, the child's literature and environment — are fine-tuned to improve the child's natural talent and their development in life's various circumstances, then the child's education is successful and beneficial.* When, on the contrary, the child's natural talent is neglected, if it is not developed or refined, when the educational factors coerce them to move in direction which is alien to them by nature, (they teach them mathematics, for example, on a level far beyond the basic knowledge that they need for life), the child grows up to be an unsuccessful person.

Education is successful to the extent that it conforms to its role and fulfills its mission, directed *toward the student's inner nature*, as God created the child to be perfected, developed, refined, by means of educational factors and facilitators.

LeNetivot Yisrael (Paths of Israel) p. 6

Simply put: Every child comes into the world with a certain talent. The role of the parent/teacher is to help the child to perfect themselves, to actualize what is inherent in them, and not to impose unnecessary studies or memorization on them.

Look how much responsibility rests with the educator, for they have to identify exactly what the uniqueness of the child is, to ensure that their natural inclination and talents are pointed in the right direction, and to help them to direct their time and energies to the proper objective.

But what if I have ten children, each one of whom is different and special?

Look at the following quotation:

When "well-read educators" come, look at the exterior of the child, (and relate to them as non-listening/noisy) and are oblivious to the child's essential self, (they don't perceive the child's uniqueness), they add straw to the fire, and make things worse (How so?) They give the thirsty vinegar to drink, (instead of pure water to nourish the seeds), the brain and the heart of the child are force-fed with everything that is alien to them (math or dumb TV), and the child's essential "me" is forgotten, and since there is no *"me,"* there is no *"Him"* (contact with the Higher Power), and certainly there is no *"you,"* the other.

Rav A.Y. Kook, Orot HaKodesh (Lights of Holiness) 3:149

The Grand Rabbi of Pietzsana (location), a small Polish town, wrote:

> The educator who wants to discover the soul of the student, which is hidden and concealed within him, in order to elevate it and set it on fire, so that it will burn with a heavenly and holy fire... must bow before the student he educates and penetrate into his smallness and his lowliness, until he reaches the spark of his hidden, even vanished, soul, to extract it, to make it grow, and to enlarge it.

The Students' Obligation, 8

So what is the uniqueness of this child?
When does the child bloom? When do they wither?
What makes them cooperate?
What can you do to enrich the area in which they excel?

Bad child?

The child doesn't listen, doesn't cooperate, they're in their own world, they're not focused. In our days, a child like this is drugged with Ritalin. Rav Kook looks at this child completely differently:

> The *really great* people find inner conflict within themselves regarding learning internal resistance to learning, because everything lives *within them* and is transformed from their spirit, and they must always be deep in their inner spirit, and the learning aspect is only auxiliary and secondary to them, and the main factor to perfect is *their* Torah, their own private Torah, as it says in Psalms, "And

he will ponder *his* Torah day and night," (that is, his own, private Torah, which his heart desires to learn, rather than what the educational system forces him to desire.) Sometimes one does not know his own worth, and turns his back on his own Torah, (without really connecting to the Torah he learns, and desires to be "scholarly," because of other people's common practice), or the appeal of some scholarly logical argument. (Instead of connecting the Torah to himself, he treats it as something external to him), and then the painful descent begins to darken the world of these great but weak people.

Clouds of Purity, 61

Rabbi Kook also writes in the book *Orot Hakodesh* (*Lights of Holiness*):

Each person builds his spiritual world *for himself, within himself*. The attribute of listening is a way to prepare the eternal building of *the individual's* own self (and not to learn concepts, to be tested on them, and to forget them.) *All Torah study is the study of "the verse of the person's first name"* (that is, the Torah which relates to him directly, as an individual)... and sometimes, listening is so intrusive, that he loses his self-concentration.

And Rabbi Kook concludes with a shocking sentence, but one which unfortunately very clearly describes someone who has lost their own uniqueness:

He knows many names (other people's theories), but he has forgotten his own name.

Volume 3, page 139

You understand? What does a child who fails to be meaningful do? Who fails to leave a mark? Who isn't smart enough to be the smartest in the class? The answer is, they leave a negative mark.

The message is simple: the moment you help a child to realize their abilities, they will be successful, but if you try to put them into an educational system that doesn't belong to them, you create a permanent sense of failure in them: they'll disturb the class, they'll dream, they won't let the teacher teach.

Who really believes that a chemical drug, one that makes changes in children's brains, is the solution? Who really thinks that stigmatizing a third of the younger generation is progress/ the wonders of science, or any other positive definition? Who doesn't realize that this is the biggest sham of the twentieth century, that drug companies invented a disease that doesn't exist in order to sell a drug to cure it? According to my worldview, someone who really preaches to parents that Ritalin is comparable to eyeglasses, and that if parents deny it to their child they are denying them essential and basic support, is confused and lost, and promoters of Ritalin drag hundreds of thousands of pure souls down with them.

What's needed is an educational worldview that sees the child and their mission. That's it. Before it's too late. May this book help educators, who certainly understand more than I do about educating children, to develop a model for finding the child's uniqueness, a model that fits the educational systems of our generation.

A Word to Managers and Administrators

Does worker X in organization Y want to leave their mark? The answer seems to be self-evident. Every worker, wherever they may be, even the lowest-ranking one, wants to feel significant, to feel that their opinion will be listened to and influence decision-making. Frustrated workers are ones who can't make an impression, who discover that their efforts to improve and streamline the workplace are unappreciated. They feel trivialized, they know that they will leave no mark; they feel like a "passing shadow," like "just anybody" who works somewhere and one day will be replaced.

Many organizations are concerned about stimulating and motivating their workers. They hire lots of organizational consultants and conduct workshops for managers and workers, without asking even for a minute the main question: What motivates people? Why is the CEO of the company motivated? Why are managers motivated? The answer to motivating workers is simple: if we would enable each worker to leave their mark on the organization, to feel significant, we would generate a highly motivated worker with great vision, a can-do attitude, who has initiative and comes to work with a smile and a lot of desire to achieve.

When people go to work and feel bad there, they become

bad workers.

Conclusion: There is no bad worker, there's just a worker who's not in the right place and who's not in a position that suits their personality and abilities. If we give them a different job, isn't there a chance that they would flourish? It's just like a puzzle — the fact you can't put a piece in a place not intended for it doesn't make the piece superfluous or invalid. It just shows that you haven't yet found the right place for it.

So that's what I want to say to managers, in a nutshell: There's no bad worker, there's just a worker who isn't in his or her appropriate job or position.

To See Ourselves as Messengers

How do we begin to connect with the messenger within us?

You get up in the morning and go to some working place. In front of a computer or in the field, as a teller in the bank, or as a waitress in a restaurant, an actor on the stage, or any other job. It doesn't matter what job you getting up for, you're already emissaries.

A taxi driver drives people from place to place. He could get up in the morning with the thought "Ugh, another day, a nightmare, when will it be over?" or he can get up with the thought "Here, I have another chance to give of myself to people, to others. I have a chance to make an impact on them by what I do, to drive them from one place to another, and I have an opportunity to make them smile, to help an old woman with a heavy bag from the grocery store."

Don't wait until you're perfect to begin to be messengers.

This example, the taxi driver, I had just made up, but it turns out that it's real. On Gett Taxi's Facebook page, a customer by the name of Hagit Gidron posted the following letter in July, 2015:

I can't believe there are such people. This morning, I ordered a Gett Taxi in Ashkelon. I opened the door and sat in the back seat. I was in the middle of a phone call, expecting the ride to start, but the driver didn't move. I didn't understand why and just muttered: "To the train station," but the driver still didn't move. I raised my head and looked at him. I almost started to get angry, but then I saw that I was in a cab decorated with butterflies: on the roof, the seats, the whole cab was filled with butterflies. I was so shocked I hung up. "I don't move anywhere without making sure my clients feel content and comfortable," the driver said, handing me a classic strawberry-flavored candy. Apparently, this is a person who sees their profession as a real mission, and not just as simply transporting people from place to place. They see themselves as uplifting passengers from a low point to a point where their day is happy. And to remind me that I was happy, the driver gave me a hairpin in the shape of a butterfly as a souvenir. So Gett Taxi — thank you for sending me Joshua Butterflies.

When a person makes an impact, through their talent, on others, when they give them what they're in need of, at that moment they repair themselves.

There are stutterers who are singers; while they sing, their stuttering miraculously disappears. The pleasure they give others by singing repairs themselves.

Hodaya thought: First I'll deal with my bulimia and then I can help other girls. That's logical, isn't it? That depends on what logic. God answers: My foolish daughter, start helping other girls, and that will correct your bulimia.

I could tell myself, first fix yourself, fix your weight and diet 100%, and then lecture to others and write books. God will answer me in the same way: Foolish man, if you only deal with fixing yourself, you will remain stuck inside of yourself, and it's reasonable to assume that no repair will come out of it.

Imagine a world in which we all feel that way, without cynicism, without money blinding us so that we don't see the other. Give to others; if you choose to be a loyal messenger instead of a self-centered egoist, the money will come anyway.

This isn't an illusion, but an accurate description of what will be uncovered when we change our consciousness; thus, all of reality, both private and social, will be elevated.

Most people think that in order for us to be good as a society, a miracle or a cosmic change must happen here. That isn't so. The only change needed is in our consciousness.

In any event, you're messengers, whether you like it or not. Now it remains for everyone to put themselves in their mission's place, and give it their all.

What does the life of a person with mission-consciousness life look like? How do they live?

I'll tell you about myself.

I believe I was sent here to do a job, so I start the morning with thanksgiving to the Higher Power: I thank you, living King, for compassionately restoring my soul, *Your faith is great*, for my life was restored to me again as a gift, and many opportunities (which are both a privilege and an obligation) were presented to me to impact and act, and He, the Higher Power, *believes in me* that I will fulfill my mission. Immediately after the prayer, I enter into a routine of activity out of a sense that there is no one else in the world that can do what I'm doing. I write books, meet people, prepare lessons, and lecture to thousands. My wife and daughters are part of the mission, too; they also need me. In the course of all this, I pay taxes, because it's my duty, and because it's also part of my mission to the State and society. In the middle of all this, I exercise and prepare healthy food for myself, to take care of the messenger. Eating is also a mission, whether viewed from the viewpoint of the cosmos, how you're fed and feed others without harming anything, living in peace with the planet, or whether you look at it from the viewpoint of the mysticism of the Torah that claims that when we eat, we elevate the plant or animal to the level of man because they become part of us. Yesterday I ate a cucumber, and today that cucumber becomes the energy with which I write this book. Thus, the cucumber I ate became part of the book.

Meanwhile, I'm assisted by other emissaries. One came to fix my washing machine, the second, a naturopathic nutritionist, made me a menu, and the third, whom all of us would call a "messenger," brought me a package from the post office...

In the middle of the day, someone cuts me off on the road, and instead of getting angry, I ask myself, "What mission did come to do for me now?"

Most of the day of the messenger is in general happy, for someone who lives in a state of mission-consciousness isn't so dependent on others, on their responses, on whether they say a good word or not. They receive a lot of power just by virtue of fulfilling their mission.

Just before my eyes close and my soul is released from the bonds of this world, I give thanks for the mission, I forgive anyone who hurt me, one way or the other, I abandon thoughts about the day and the plans for tomorrow, and I connect to the Higher Power . Not just my cellphone needs charging.

THE MISSION MAP

I will try to graphically combine the insights we honed in order to assemble all the parts of the puzzle into a clear mission map that will help you implement your mission as soon as possible.

To this end, we will use as an example the story of Moriah's mission:

Moriah came to me with a great desire to find her mission. She's a thirty-two-year-old lawyer who hated her job, and so she left the lawyers' office in which she worked for several years after she got her law degree. Now she works as a personal trainer in gyms.

Remember what we said about the environment, what it signals to you, how it confirms you? I asked her what her environment was signaling to her. She replied that the surroundings were positively signaling her interest in sports and the subject of "giving charity secretly." Every Passover and Rosh Hashana, she and another friend organize dozens of packages for the needy. In addition, she told a surprising story: "My friends signal me, almost on a daily basis, that I help them with their relationships." I was very surprised. Moriah is single and, according to what she told me, she didn't herself experience too many serious and long-lasting relationships. Her friends, on the other hand, are married. "How exactly do you help your married girlfriends with their marriages?" I asked her.

"My mother and father," she said, "have been married for nearly forty years. They love each other, but fight all the time." I felt her choking on her tears. "That's the most painful thing in my life," she said. (Isn't this an example of failure?) "I remember seeing my father depressed, and I would ask him what had happened. He would answer that everything was fine. But I, from a young age, realized something bad was happening. This made me very sensitive, very sharp."

"When my friends tell me about themselves, I immediately think about how my father felt, and I faithfully present the side of their husband that they don't see, and so I manage to open a window for them to the other side's feelings. I think that's why they give me feedback that their conversations with me help them."

"That's amazing," I told her, "Nothing in this world is unnecessary. The Higher Source sent you precisely these parents to train you and to prepare you for a mission, for what you can give to the world.

"Does helping them do you any good?" I asked

"It's the best thing in the world," she replied. "There is nothing in the world that makes me happier."

Did that ring a bell to figure out her mission only for me? Can you see her mission too?

I sent Moriah to a take a course in mediation. She invested in setting up a website, wrote articles, and printed up business cards. She became a real professional.

There's another issue that I pointed out to her: "When couples come to me and our mediation fails, and the couple decides to divorce, our meetings have come to an end, since I don't know family law. You, however, *are* a lawyer, and thus you can give couples who come to you much more than I can.

You're both a mediator and an attorney. You can help them try to save their marriage, but if that doesn't succeed, you can also help them divorce amicably, in an honorable way, without waging war on each other.

I've included Moriah's answers in this table, as examples to help you fill in your own answers:

Goal	Example	Your answer
I would most want to help people who:	Are couples who don't succeed in communicating	
All my life I dreamed of and wanted:	That my parents would stop fighting, and that I would have a better marriage than them	
I'm good at:	Sports, management, mediation, encouragement, human relations, being precise about the truth	
My social environment asks for my help in:	Relationships, sports, anonymous charity	

Goal	Example	Your answer
My social environment gives me positive feedback when:	I help my friends with their problems in their marriages	
I'm the most fulfilled when I:	Help people who are lacking/ for whom things are difficult	
I struggle for many years with/I fail at/it's hard for me to:	My relationships, my parents' relationship	
I have degrees in/ I learned	Law and marital mediation	
After reading this book and doing the exercises, my sense is that my mission is almost certainly:	Marital mediation	

To Sum Up the Journey

If you're one of the people who read the book and, like many, you saw that you're already carrying out a great mission, but you never called it this big, fancy word — you're blessed. It's great to know that you're in the right place. I'm sure that this awareness will greatly strengthen you.

If you're a practical person, who just needs to know "what" and the "how" already flows by itself, and the book helped you to pinpoint the answer to the question of your mission in the world — you're really fortunate. Go and succeed, and have an impact on the whole world.

But if you're still debating, if the direction isn't perfectly clear, and the thought of concrete practical steps is frightening and paralyzing, if the questions are still around: So what should I do about my mission in the world? I read the book, connected to it, I did the exercises and even I think that I know what my mission is. What now? What do you recommend that I do? What's the right thing to do? Quit my job and go "all the way" with the dream? Should I wait? And how will I know that I have come to the most accurate conclusion?

First of all, be happy, you're in good company. Even Rabbi Kook grappled with the same indecisions:

What should I do, with what should I concern myself? Is

a perpetually stable, unvaried activity appropriate for me,
or one that leaps, jumps, changes, and sways?

His Rooms, **130**

If you reached the end of the book and your mission is on your agenda, it means that you're on track, that the path is clear, that the chaos or the self-abandonment is over. But while in some people, the change occurs very quickly, in others it happens more slowly. But don't worry, it *will* happen. At your own pace.

I would like to conclude with a few practical tips that may help you:

a. Read the book again, and be sure to do the exercises.

b. Don't be shy to ask for help from me or from other professionals in the field. Any experienced personal trainer can help you, especially after the process you have undergone by reading this book.

c. Your fears are there to work with and clarify things, not for you to skip over, and certainly not to paralyze you.

d. Stop comparing yourself to others. Excellence occurs when people succeed for themselves.

e. You don't run the world. Let the real Manager, "He Who spoke and the world was created," do His part; this will both free you up to do just your own part, and will also help you avoid perfectionism.

f. In the spirit of the tip above - please erase tasks, abandon things, say no to assignments, release yourself from duties, delegate authority, etc. Most people just load up upon themselves, mentally and physically, a lot more than one person can handle alone, so they aren't free to perform their mission. Unloading a burden of thoughts and tasks from yourself is almost a mitzvah. Ask yourself — what will happen if I don't do this? Won't things be okay anyway?

g. Your success is the success of all of us. Your mission is essential for all humanity. It's not just between you and your bank account, or just between you and your self-confidence. So let's go — get going on your mission; everyone is waiting.

Final Words

And Jacob went out from Beersheba, and went toward Haran. And he came to a certain place, and stayed there all night, because the sun had set; and he took some of the stones of that place, and put them under his head, and lay down in that place to sleep. And he dreamed, and behold, a ladder was set up on the earth, and the top of it reached heaven: and behold, the angels of God were ascending and descending on it. And, behold, the Lord stood above him.

Genesis 28:10-13

Yaakov Avinu (our father Jacob), the Torah says in Genesis 28, dreamed of angels going up and down the ladder. Why, our Sages ask, why are the angels first going up and only then going down the ladder? Why aren't they doing down first and only then going up? And anyway, what is the interpretation of one of the most famous dreams in history? Rabbi Samson Raphael Hirsch interprets this passage as follows:

> Yaakov sees that man's fate isn't determined on earth, in the physical world of the senses, he sees the emissaries of God. "Angel" (Hebrew, *malach*) in the sense of work

(Hebrew: *m'lacha*, someone who does work is called an angel. That is to say, angels are messengers, too, not only we are, the difference being that angels have no freedom of choice and we do.) And behold, they look at the ideal image of man, as he should be, and go down and compare it to his image as he actually is, and to this extent they confront him, for better or for worse. And so they were, as the Sages say, "Ascending and looking at the heavenly image, and descending and looking at the earthly image" They come with a knife to stab him lightly so that he would wake up... "and they went down and found him asleep." He slept in a place that was supposed to give him thoughts of his mission, and direct him towards that supreme goal.

(Rabbi Samson Raphael Hirsch, Genesis 28)

Each of us, according to Rabbi Hirsch, has a picture they don't know about, an ideal picture, a situation with great potential that hasn't yet been discovered. The angels ascend to check the ideal picture, and descend and look at the actual person. They find them asleep, they compare the images, they don't understand why the person doesn't progress towards the ideal image. They don't understand why they are strewn around, distracted, preoccupied with everything that they are not, occupied with escaping from the mission. They, the angels, have no choice: they stab the person lightly with a knife; they try to make them wake up.

This guide, **Who You Were Meant to Be**, is preventive medicine for you; it will prevent the stab of the knife that is meant for you. Fulfill what is written in the book, and when the angels come and recall your ideal image, they will find you doing your job faithfully, making sure to give to others what only you can give. They will find you faithful messengers.

When the angels come and compare the two pictures, they will have no choice but to say: This is the person. This is the picture we saw there, up above.

It's Good to Give Thanks

First and foremost, to the Almighty, He Who spoke and the world was created.

Even were my mouth as full of song as the sea is full of water, and my lips as full of poetry as its multitude of waves, and my tongue full of joy, and my hands spread out like the eagles of heaven, and my feet as light as a deer, all these wouldn't suffice to allow me to describe the righteousness of God, everything He did, is doing, and will do, and my words wouldn't suffice to thank Him for all the grace and help He gave me. I can't understand why He does so much for me, far beyond what I deserve; perhaps because there is no time left to waste, and our generation deserves, and is obligated, to deal with the issue of mission.

To everyone who has gone on the journey with me to the ensure accuracy of the guide you have in your hands: Anat Lev Adler, Rivka Goldberg, Hannah Ovadia, Sharon Ofir, Efrat Mani, Nir Klauberg, and Dana Ariel.

To Dr. Simcha Leibowitz, for granting me the privilege to help him develop the idea of leaving a mark, and for the mark he made on me.

To Rabbi Assaf Moshe Beiler, who is a walking inspiration to me.

To Oded, Simone, and Esther, who agreed to be your inspiration and mine, and to be interviewed for this book.

To Eran Stern, for the excellent opening remarks.

To Sharon Eizen, who "kicked me" to write.

To Hodaya, Inbal, and Sivan, for making things real.

To Yael Shachnai, who was apparently sent to me as a faithful emissary on the way to publication.

To the knowledge in this book that isn't mine — thank you for choosing to pass to others through me.

To my wife — I couldn't exist without her.

To contact Moshe, email him at sharon@mo6.co.il.

Made in the USA
Middletown, DE
07 July 2019